WHIRLWIND

JOURNEYS WITH JOB THROUGH GRIEF, ANXIETY, AND PAIN

by

Wesley M. Eades

Milton P. Horne

Cover art by Joel Edwards (www.jredwardsstudios.com)

ISBN: 1480202789

ISBN-13: 9781480202788

Library of Congress Control Number: 2013902241

CreateSpace Independent Publishing Platform

North Charleston, South Carolina

DEDICATION

This book is dedicated to all of our brothers and sisters who have stood in the whirlwind of numbing grief, anxiety and pain.

We are walking together.

Lord have mercy.
Christ have mercy.

TABLE OF CONTENTS

ACKNOWLEDGMENTS

I am truly grateful to William Jewell College for the sabbatical in the spring of 2012 that allowed me to complete my part of the work on this book. I am also grateful for many friends who have faithfully read parts of the book and commented on it. I especially thank members of my adult Bible study class at the Second Baptist Church, Liberty, Missouri. Nothing has ever challenged me quite like reading the instructional literature of the Hebrew Bible, and I thank all those who have patiently listened to me talk about it over the years.

MILTON

I cannot express enough appreciation for the hundreds of clients who have challenged my small self and encouraged the formation of my Authentic Self over the years. I'm particularly grateful for those of you who have been reading and commenting on this project over the past several months. I am also so thankful for my wife, Holly, who has supported many of my projects, several of which have been of questionable value!

WES

INTRODUCTION

This book is about telling the truth in religious faith.

We hold the assumption that real spiritual transformation occurs when people move from expecting God to take care of them, to realizing that peace is possible regardless of circumstances. Our observation is that people often use religion to try to control the uncontrollable, which, in turn, magnifies suffering. We believe that the mature journey of faith is a path to accepting reality as it presents itself.

We address several aspects of the mature spiritual journey by presenting thirty homilies on the biblical book of Job. Each homily is then followed by a fictional pastoral counseling session. These sessions are intended to portray individuals grappling with the challenges of being honest about faith while retaining faith. This religious honesty is more challenging than people usually admit.

We assume that virtually all ministers both preach and counsel, and we further believe that preaching and counseling are two of the primary ways that ministers help congregations learn how to read and interpret the Bible. However, our observation is that many, if not most, regular church attendees still struggle deeply with what it means to live out faith in the midst of suffering. Bible study classes seldom raise the hardest questions about faith. In fact, and this will seem judgmental on our part, such classes are often only interested in a biblical book in a superficial way. We do not deny the importance of individual study, of course. But we have found that most who practice faith, especially faith in the midst of crises, rely heavily upon their ministers to set out for them the thrust of the biblical story in the context of worship and counseling.

The Book of Job and the Person in the Pew

We hope this book can be of help to ministers; however, our central aim is to address laypersons directly. Two reasons guide our thinking.

First, the book of Job is vitally important for addressing the challenge of holding on to faith while questioning faith. Given this, we find it puzzling that the book of Job is simply not that important in Christian (or Jewish) worship. Only rarely are readings from Job included in Christian lectionaries or prayer books. For Christians in the Free Church tradition (thus not relying upon lectionaries or the Book of Common Prayer), when was the last time you heard in worship a reading or a sermon from the book of Job? Ministers rarely draw from the book of Job in their preaching, teaching, and counseling. Thus Christian worshippers are very unlikely to learn the book in any detail. And yet, we believe this is one of the theologically most important books in the Christian canon, especially in light of the Christian story of Jesus.

The second reason we wish to address laypersons concerns what happens in Christian preaching. Or, we should say, what does not happen, at least not much. Worshippers rarely talk about sermons, at least not beyond the compulsory *I liked it, or it was off today.* It is rare to find worshippers reflecting thoughtfully upon the substance of the minister's sermon. Oh, to be sure, congregants might comment upon an example or an application, especially if it gets too political. But seldom do worshippers talk with each other about sermons relating to the challenge of holding faith when nearly everything around congregants challenges it. What is more, it is increasingly difficult for worshippers to share with each other at any level of depth. Deepest struggles are reserved for ministers in counseling sessions, rather than other congregants. Such absence of conversation is related to a number of realities, we know, including the rather superficial level of trust that is maintained within communities of faith. But the simple lack of knowledge of the biblical story also contributes to this lack of deep sharing and conversation. And so, the fictional counseling sessions in this book model the exchange of ideas that grow from and are related to a collection of homilies on the book of Job.

Since there are thirty homilies, we go beyond the most well-known parts of Job's story. We include texts that most readers of the book of

Job probably never think about. For this reason, preaching becomes a means of offering an interpretation of the book of Job. And we invite our readers into a conversation about a theologically rich book. We also invite them to engage in the challenge of being honest about holding to religious faith.

WHAT IS A HOMILY?

Some readers might be more comfortable with the word *sermon* instead of *homily*. Such a sentiment would be consistent with our (the authors') backgrounds. As we learned Christian faith growing up, a homily simply meant a very short sermon. But the term homily has a much more interesting past.

In the New Testament, the verbal form of the word behind *homily* (something analogous to *homilize*) occurs in Luke 24:14. It denotes that the disciples were *talking to each other* as they were on their way to Emmaus. Thus, if the noun form is related, a homily simply denotes a conversation. One of the great challenges of preaching is making sermons conversational. Origen, one of Christianity's early Alexandrian theologians (183–253 CE), insisted that a homily was to take place in a worship setting, to be derived from scripture, and to continue the idea of conversation about scripture[1]. The so-called homilies presented here are somewhat in-line with this tradition. Although they have never been used in worship, they are grounded in scripture and seek to be in conversation about the ideas in scripture. They seek to promote conversation in three ways: First, these homilies use everyday language and examples to communicate. Second, the fictional therapy sessions portray further one context in which conversation might continue. And third, we hope the deeper connections between homilies and counseling sessions will inspire ongoing conversations among readers of the book.

We are aware that interpreting the book of Job presents challenges for modern Christian preachers. While the stories of Jesus' life and that of Job have much in common, it may be difficult to understand those

---

[1] J. Kevin Coyle, "From Homily to Sermon to Homily: The Content of Christian Liturgical Preaching in Historical Perspective." *Liturgical Ministry* (Winter 2000): 1–9.

commonalities from a Christian point of view. In fact, the homilies presented here are not explicitly concerned with the Christian gospel *per se.* Their subject matter does not necessarily elevate the core Christian claims. They do make intersections with the Christian story at many points. They are probably much more broadly related, though, to Christian practice through their focus on personal moral behavior and emotional development.

THE COUNSELING SESSIONS: BECOMING AN AUTHENTIC SELF

Wes's *pastoral anthropology*, that is, his view of human nature, is grounded in the Christian tradition. Wes assumes that human beings are created out of God's love, but they must live in a creation that has been tragically corrupted. Therefore, all persons live with a fundamental unrest—or anxiety. All of the world's great religious traditions agree on at least one core point: Human beings experience deep inner conflict. This dilemma is perhaps no more simply described in Christian scripture than by the Apostle Paul's confession in the book of Romans, chapter 7, vs.15: *I do not understand my own actions. For I do not do what I want, but I do the very thing I hate.*

Paul goes on to describe the battle between the spiritual nature and the carnal nature. Many writers have offered language to capture this experience. The terms *True Self* and *False Self,* for instance, have been popular among spiritual seekers for years. However, we will address these concepts using Burt Burleson's *Authentic Self* and *small self.*[2]

We believe the term *False Self* suggests an inaccurately negative judgment. The term *small self,* however, reflects our belief that persons carry an anxious passenger that is not so much *bad* as confusing and immature. This is not to deny that some people behave in ways that seem completely *evil* and destructive, but only to say that the universal labeling of the small self as evil is unwarranted.

Furthermore, we have found that many religious circles hold the misguided belief that the small self must be virtually beaten into submission, if not destroyed. We argue that, while the small self is

---

[2] See "The Authentic Self" at http://www.wmeades.com/authself.htm.

certainly a bearer of our wounds and anxieties, it also is a source of great joy and energy. The goal of spiritual formation is to strengthen the Authentic Self and to love the small self well.

We also know that selfhood in general is much more complex than we can set out here. Nevertheless, a common misunderstanding is that the human intellectual self is somehow separate from the human emotional self, and thus people frequently emphasize rationality over emotion. We want to stress that emotion, intuition, feeling, attitude, mood, etc. are fundamental to intellection. Spirituality and religious faith educate the emotions by transforming them from mere self-centered survival mechanisms to facilitators of personal wholeness and social cohesiveness.[3]

HOW TO READ THIS BOOK

The texts for each homily have been selected as readers might encounter them in reading through the book of Job from beginning to end. The aim is to create a "homiletic reading" of the entire book of Job. The homilies generally reflect the development of Job's story. Some homilies offer special focus on particular themes, however, and seem more to stand on their own without connecting to the flow of the narrative.

The homilies never exceed seven hundred words and can be read in a few minutes (or preached in under ten minutes). We are not suggesting they be read that quickly, though. The homilies themselves require careful reflection. The clinical scenarios are comparable but are necessarily a bit longer in order to develop crucial applications of ideas that might emerge in real conversation. The aim of reading the two together is to evoke conversation about both the book of Job and the role of religious faith in becoming healthy individuals.

The homilies include focal biblical texts that provoke the main ideas treated in the body. Unless otherwise indicated, we use the New Revised Standard Version of the Bible in quotations from scripture. You may find it beneficial to use your own Bible to examine the larger contexts

---

[3] Paraphrasing the work of Loyal Rue, *Religion Is Not about God: How Spiritual Traditions Nurture Our Biological Nature and What to Expect When They Fail* (New Brunswick, NJ and London: Rutgers University Press, 2005), 78–124.

in which each focal text functions. Each unit contains both an initial *Connections* section and a *Reflections* section. While these two sections are intended to assist and guide readers' reflections, they are not intended to be exhaustive or prescriptive.

Creating counseling narratives from actual counseling relationships can be tricky. An experienced counselor—or any highly intuitive person, for that matter—will no doubt find the narratives a bit too *clean* to reflect reality. There's no question that Wes has, at times, compressed insights that often occur over a few sessions into a single conversation. All of the narratives are, though, very true to real relationships with real people.

There Was a Man from the Land of Uz

Job 1:1

There was once a man in the land of Uz whose name was Job. That man was blameless and upright, one who feared God and turned away from evil.

Connections

Why have you picked up this book?

Perhaps you are a pastor wondering if we've found a way to add some clarity to a confusing book in the Bible.

Maybe you are a layperson with higher-than-average interest in biblical studies.

Or, could it be you are looking for anything that might help you get through another painful day?

We want to help you in all these ways, but we especially want to help you be honest—honest about yourself, honest about the book of Job, and honest about God.

The book of Job raises timeless questions about the meaning of life and about what we can expect of God as we struggle. Themes of mystery, justice, theology, and community weave through this ancient story in much the same way they weave through our own stories. Milton, through his homilies, will help you understand what the book actually says, and doesn't say, about such things. Wes, through fictional, though reality-based, counseling narratives, will help you see how these themes continually stir us up in the practical challenges of life.

Before continuing, we recommend a brief exercise. Consider these first three verses from Job:

> *There was once a man in the land of Uz whose name was Job. That man was blameless and upright, one who feared God and turned away from evil. There were born to him seven sons and three daughters. He had seven thousand sheep, three thousand camels, five hundred yoke of oxen, five hundred donkeys, and very many servants; so that this man was the greatest of all the people of the east.*

Now ask yourself: What would these opening verses say if they were about you? If you had to capture "me" in only three sentences, what would those sentences be? We recommend you jot down your sentences on the page at the beginning of this chapter.

THE HOMILY

We are reminded of the universality of suffering almost on a daily basis. When was the last time you heard of some horrible plight coming upon some person or her family in some place far removed from your community? It probably hasn't been that long, thanks to the Internet and the constant watch of anyone who has an electronic communication device with video capabilities. And, having all that information, do you care about it anymore? In fact, I wonder whether contemporary capabilities to know moment by moment who's suffering in the world (as well as who's winning the *daily pick three*) does not actually make it all rather mundane, routine, and therefore uninteresting. Reports about some horrific disaster around the world flash across either our television screens or our cell phones every moment. They flash into our thoughts and as quickly evaporate as the next bit of data appears on the screen.

One of the things that makes this story of Job so fascinating to me is the apparent anonymity of the main character, Job. Why should we care about him? And I don't think this is only a problem for the contemporary reader, but it would have been for the ancient reader, too. The opening line of the story tells us that Job came from a place called *Uz*. Ever wonder if ancient readers asked the same thing we do: *Where the heck is that?* Members of ancient audiences would have needed to be fairly scripturally literate to know that Uz is mentioned in Lamentations 4:21: *Rejoice and be glad, O daughter of Edom, that you live in the land of Uz.* And the literate audience members may have known that the land of Edom was the object of at least one prophet's wrath—Obadiah 1–4. But who knew anything about Obadiah?

Maybe an ancient reader only needed to know that this story did *not* take place in the land of Israel. Perhaps *Uz* was the poet's way of saying that such things could not, and would not, ever happen in the homeland. It's like one of those comforting fictions that contemporary folk entertain about the *land of the free*, even though they are actually living in a culture that perpetuates its own kinds of slaveries. Job was not an Israelite, so how could his suffering concern me? In fact, it's not just that he and his friends were foreigners, but he lived so long ago, didn't he? Don't the opening lines have that *once-upon-a-time* feel to them? I mean, he reminds you of Abraham, somewhat, doesn't he? His wealth is in land, animals, and big family. He's the religious leader of the clan, the one who offers sacrifices, just like Abraham. And, for that matter, was Abraham even a Hebrew? Didn't he come from Ur of the Chaldeans (Genesis 11:31)? And yet, Abraham is like the patriarch of all persons of Jewish, Christian, and Muslim faith, isn't he? Citing Abraham is one of the ways that the *big three* monotheistic religions say, *yes*, we have something in common.

3

Maybe that is all we need to know when it comes to suffering. As Abraham was the patriarch of ethical monotheism, perhaps Job's *long-ago-and-far-away* background is given so we will think of him as a kind of patriarch of suffering. That way suffering is not just localized in the life of an unknown person. Rather, because he's my father in some sense, his suffering is mine, too. (Jesus should probably work that way for Christians, but I'm afraid he's so much our Christ that we forget that he was a man, too.) No matter where suffering occurs, or to whom, it is a part of my inheritance, a part of my story. In fact, like a patriarchal lineage, I cannot disown it or deny it. Suffering is a part of my bloodline, defining what it means to be a person of faith. When I hear of anyone suffering, because we are all descendants of Job, it is a family member who is suffering. Suffering is not anonymous, thanks to my being a part of the family of Job.

JANIE

Somewhere, somehow, we began to live as if we were separate, alone, and in danger. Once afraid, we constructed a self out of that fear and have been steadfastly defending it ever since.

KABIR HELMINSKI, *LIVING PRESENCE*

"But if I don't do a PhD, then won't I just be settling for less than I can be?"

For Janie this is a desperate question. Her eyes express the terror of a cornered animal. For all her work in therapy, her traumatized brain can still get hooked by the small-self whisper: *You'll never measure up.* I think about the open lines of Job and wonder how Janie's life might be captured in less than one hundred words:

There was a young woman from East Texas whose name was Janie. She was a gifted therapist who wanted to please God. Having survived a childhood of abuse and neglect, Janie graduated from college with a master's degree in counseling. Her outstanding work with juvenile offenders allowed her to create a life of wealth compared to her beginnings. Janie could confront an angry teen about his self-defeating choices, only to have that same boy begging her to play basketball with the "inmates" later the same afternoon. Janie was considered the best in town at her work.

"Janie, where is that question coming from? Is it your small self pushing you toward another degree, or your Authentic Self? I'd never want to dampen your urge to study, but it has taken you years to create a life characterized more by meaning than by suffering. Why would you want to heap more stress upon yourself now?"

"I don't know. I don't know." Janie's eyes are pleading. "It just seems like I ought to go for the PhD. What? You don't think I could do it?"

"Of course you could do it. Listen to yourself for a moment. What are you feeling? You seem to be frantic right now. What's going on? Help me understand."

Janie leans back, "When is my small self going to just shut up? I know you're right. The kids were all high-fiving me last night when I played basketball with them. By ten o'clock I'd turned myself into a total mess. Even with all my meds I couldn't sleep. I just kept thinking about what a loser I was for not having a PhD, like you. My Authentic Self tries to remind me of all I've accomplished, but it's like it doesn't matter."

"Let's go back to basics for a moment. Your wounded small self is never going to simply go away. You've done such great work in strengthening your God-breathed Authentic Self, but the small self is never going to give up easily."

"Then what's the point of all this?"

"You tell me."

I get the patented Janie eye-roll before she answers.

"I get one shot at this life. I can either run with it or live my life like a victim."

"You've been running with it and creating something out of almost nothing. But it still doesn't feel like enough, does it?"

"Not on days like today."

I notice that the frantic look has faded from Janie's eyes. She seems more present now.

"I think I told you my friend Milton and I are working on a book about Job. Parts of it keep popping into my mind during my sessions."

"Yeah. I've started reading it again. I hope you weren't expecting me to be encouraged by *that* story."

"That's a fair dig." I hope my smile reflects the tenderness I feel. "I guess most of us would find more encouragement in what we *think* the story says. Some guy loses everything, and then God makes sure he gets it back. But what I'm thinking right now is that you are almost the anti-Job. You started with nothing, have created a stunning life, and yet still find yourself on the trash heap on a regular basis."

"Are you saying I'm doing this to myself?" Is that a hint of fire in those eyes?

"OK, did you notice how you automatically assumed I was thinking the worst of you?" I'm leaning forward now. "You and I both understand now what an upbringing like yours does to a brain. Constant survival pressures on the small self never allow the Authentic Self breathing room to grow. Despite this, you've slowly taken responsibility for your life. But all those old feelings of fear and hopelessness are still in your brain, and they are easily triggered."

"See? Right now I can hear what you are saying, and it makes sense." Janie curls up in a ball against the corner of my worn out couch. "But in the middle of the night, when you are not there, it's like I have amnesia."

"I know. Maybe that's why the book of Job has been around for so long. No matter how each of our stories can seem different from his, we all end up on the trash heap, angry and hopeless."

"Do you?"

"You know I do, Janie. You know a fair amount of my story. We both know what it's like to feel angry and hopeless. We both know what it's like to wonder if there is even a God out there, much less whether or not that God gives a damn."

REFLECTIONS

The opening lines of the book of Job tell us who Job is. What does it take to get us to be honest about who we are, why we choose to live the way we do, and what ultimately is of greatest value to us? Religious faith is supposed to be honest about those things, but often it is religious faith that pushes us to be the least honest.

Janie's concerns about a PhD may not seem relevant to your life. But can you see how her obsession with achievement, with the symbols of success, drives her away from her soul? Janie's life has been filled with more pain, perpetrated by others, than most. She tells herself that getting an advanced degree will somehow make things OK. Like so many of us, her suffering has slowly shifted from what has been done to her toward what she continues to do to herself.

Reading a biblical book dealing with suffering may be a curiosity to us, or it may remind us of how fear of suffering and death motivates our decision-making. And fear can be at work within us even though we are unaware of it. Where does that fear come from? And why can't we be more honest about it? How is it possible for us to bury our fears so effectively that we can be unaware of them while being influenced by them?

Being a descendant of Job is not only about physical and psychological suffering. It is about how one holds to one's religious convictions and what difference those convictions make in one's Authentic Self. Frankly, to be a descendant of Job, all you have to be is a man or woman trying to get through the day, sometimes in the face of great suffering, but always with the challenge of being honest about who you are in relationship to your convictions about God.

We probably know some of the details of Job's story. But we know much better what is happening in our own stories. Belonging to the family of Job, though, means that we have some things in common with each other as we seek to hold to faith with integrity in the experience of suffering.

2

THE CONSTANT FATHER

JOB 1:4-5

It may be that my children have sinned, and cursed God in their hearts.   .

CONNECTIONS

Can you imagine having a parent like Job? We cannot help but put ourselves in the character's shoes in some sense. And, since it's so difficult to know how the poet wanted us to read the book of Job, we just let our imaginations guide us.

It is clear, certainly, that the story of Job is not about how to raise children. The references to Job's parenting seem rather thin to pay too much attention to them. And yet, the limited information about Job and his children in the opening verses of the book may tell us something, not only about Job's parenting, but about his sense of moral conviction. This homily asks you to notice how Job attends to his grown children's behavior. We know we can attempt to control the outcomes of our own lives through religious practice; but what about the father who believes he can control the outcomes of his children's lives as well?

THE HOMILY

Job's constant attention to the moral lives of his grown children seems to be more a symptom than a virtue. Our story begins with a description of the patriarchal father who takes his role as head of house a little too seriously. We may suspect that Job believes his children's behavior might have a bearing upon his own moral reputation. But perhaps this belief is not unreasonable in the patriarchal model for persons of such rigorous piety as Abraham and Job. You may recall the story of Jacob's sons, Simeon and Levi, who deceive and then slaughter Shechem because of his impending marriage to their sister Dinah. When word of his sons' treachery reaches Jacob, he accuses them forcefully: *You have brought trouble on me by making me odious to the inhabitants of the land, the Canaanites and the Perizzites* (Genesis 34:30).

Jacob is no model of virtue; and yet even he is deeply concerned about the implications of his two sons' actions on his own reputation. But when do children finally become adults, living outside of their parents' *say-so*? When do parents finally learn to treat children as adults, letting them shoulder the moral responsibilities of adulthood without hovering over them, ever ready to swoop in and save? And do the children finally come to relate to parents as adults do to other adults? When do children no longer use parents as an excuse for how life turns for them? I ponder these questions when I discover how attentive Job was to the moral lives of his children:

...and he would rise early in the morning and offer burnt offerings according to the number of them all; for Job said, 'It may be that my children have sinned....' (1:5).

I admit it is difficult for parents to stop blaming themselves for their children's actions. The wonderful irony in Job 1:5 is that the Hebrew text actually says that Job was worried his children might have *sinned and blessed (uberaku) the Lord.* Those familiar with the book of Job will likely have been taught that the word *bless* here is simply a euphemism. If so, it might have been substituted by some pious reader (as in Job 1:11; 2:5; and 2:9) who was offended by the word *curse,* even though it seems more appropriate to the context. Yet, reading without such suspicion, it may well be that blessing could in and of itself *be* a sin, if the children sought to offer sacrifice without first being purified. But the irony is that Job sanctifies his children after their partying *not knowing* whether they intended to curse or to bless the Lord.

It is a problem for me that Job acts presumptuously in reference to his adult children's behavior. Is that what we mean by an overbearing parent? More importantly, is that what a heightened attentiveness to moral righteousness leads parents to do?

Can any one of us who also happens to have children, and possibly grandchildren, imagine how to stop such patriarchal presiding over our children's lives, short of losing them altogether?

At least two of the prophets thought about the problem of individuals being responsible for their own sins. The prophet Ezekiel condemns the idea of blaming one's circumstances on the sins of one's parents: *The parents have eaten sour grapes and the children's teeth are set on edge* (Ezekiel 18:2; Jeremiah 31:29). Bildad says as much to Job: *If your children sinned against him, he delivered them into the power of their transgression* (8:4). On the other hand, can any of us who experience the agony of Job's wife's loss of her children, *the pangs and pains of my womb which I bore in vain with sorrows* (Job 2:9, Septuagint), still think that somehow parents are not deeply involved in and responsible for their children's lives no matter how grown up they are?

BARBARA

Be very careful when caring for someone more than he cares for himself. It's a formula for great pain.

WES EADES

"I may fall asleep. Please don't take it personally; I was up all night."

"For any reason in particular?"

"Not really. I visited Brad yesterday, and that always stirs me up." What does resignation look like? At this moment it looks like Barb.

Barbara's son is in prison. Brad is twenty-seven years old, serving time for the drug lab he'd set up and used to draw the local kids toward addiction. She and her husband were active in their church, and they had made sure each of their three children attended Sunday school. Both daughters had graduated from college, married well, and are model citizens. Then there is Brad.

There's no need for details here. Suffice it to say that Brad started making destructive choices almost as soon as he hit puberty. After having raised two daughters with barely a hiccup, Barbara and her husband were not prepared for Brad's behavior. They attempted to address their concerns about their son; they took parenting classes, attended family counseling, and practiced *tough love*. No one could claim they were irresponsible in their parenting. Nonetheless, Brad is in prison, and will be there for a while.

"And what was your small self whispering to you through the night?"

"Oh, you know, the usual *parade of horribles* about what an awful mother I must be. I keep thinking we should have hired that hotshot lawyer."

"You keep thinking you should have taken out the second mortgage to pay his retainer?"

Barbara swings between a dark depression that presses her down into her mattress and an agitated anxiety that leaves her muscles aching like a marathoner's. She cannot escape the notion that she is a bad mother. She cannot release her concern for what others might be thinking. It doesn't help that her husband seems to easily find peace with Brad's choices and thinks: *He made his bed. What are we supposed to do?*

"Whenever you bring up the lawyer issue," I continue, "I'm reminded that your husband was clear about what he was, and was not, willing to do. It's not like you could have hired the guy without your husband's cooperation; yet you seem to keep returning to that decision as if it is all your fault."

"I know. It doesn't make much sense." Barbara's voice is so low. I'm not sure if she's talking to me or to herself.

How is Barbara to find peace? She readily acknowledges her faith commitments are within a tradition that insists peace is available to all, regardless of circumstances. She continually wonders what it means that she is so tortured.

"Questions without satisfying answers don't go away easily," I assure her.

"Believe me, I know. Don't you get sick of hearing me whine about where the hell God is? Aren't you tired of my endless questions about my lack of faith?" Barbara manages an exhausted smile.

"Do you think you're a whiner?"

Barbara stares out the window. "I don't think I've ever been a whiner, but I know I can sound like one these days." Her eyes turn back to mine. Her fist is gently rapping on the cushion. "It's just not right that God disappeared where my son is concerned. We *trained up our children* the right way."

Leaning in, I ask, "Surely you're not asking me to recite my little sermonette on the *failures of religious education* again."

"No, thank you. What would be the point?"

"Barb, the point is that all of your theological ruminations seem to be distracting you from the more pressing questions."

"Which questions?"

"Well, to name a few, *What sort of mother do I want to be for my incarcerated son? Am I being the mother I want to be for my daughters who seem to be living charmed lives?* And maybe even, *How do I work on a marriage with a man who wouldn't mortgage the house to the hilt in order to hire the hotshot attorney?*"

"Did someone piss in your cornflakes this morning?" Now Barbara is leaning in.

"Hey, you're not going to throw me off by getting tacky." Though I must admit I'm heartened by her sparks. I continue softly, "I'm pretty sure you're not going to get anywhere asking questions of God that will never be answered. Especially if it keeps you from asking questions you can do something about."

REFLECTIONS

During times of crisis we often discover just how dishonest we've been about our own religious faith. Like a person sitting on the side of the road with a shredded tire, we discover that we were not as prepared for the trip as we thought.

For me (Wes), this dilemma came into sharp focus my first night in the mental health unit, way back in 1998. I'd been given enough medication to put a horse into a coma, yet I was wide awake, anxiously ruminating on my dreadful circumstances. I began repeating Bible verses and prayers. When I heard myself reciting, *Now I lay me down to sleep*, it hit me. My religion was of no use to me now.

In these moments, some will conclude that they've not been good enough at religion. Such conclusions reflect continued dishonesty, and they only serve to compound guilt and shame. If you are inclined in that direction, please pause. There is another way.

One question before moving forward: *Do I really believe that my assumptions about God, and how God works in the world, are accurate and honest?*

3.

ENTICING GOD AND THE COST OF RELIGIOUS FAITH

JOB 1:8

There is no one like him on the earth, a blameless and upright man who fears God and turns away from evil.

CONNECTIONS

Have you ever been let down by someone you believed was on your side, or by someone you just *knew* you could count on? Or worse, have you ever been drawn in by someone who manipulated you into trusting him or her? The first sort of disappointment is painful, but the second sort can leave us feeling like fools. Both sorts of pain are fueled by a very common human aspect of our psychology: *expectation*.

15

It is normal for us to have expectations. You expect your car to start in the morning. You, hopefully, expect your spouse to tell you the truth when you ask a question. Expectation is a central component of religious faith. You expect God to *behave* in the ways you have been taught God would behave.

This homily paints a picture of a man who was enticed toward God through his own expectations. We can almost all relate to Job on this point. But how do we handle it when God does not seem particularly interested in fulfilling our expectations? Do we feel more manipulated *by* God in such situations, rather than enticed *toward* God? The counselor asks Frank to consider these questions.

THE HOMILY

The initial picture of God in the book of Job is enticing to us. What we don't realize is that we may be *enticed* in other, more costly, ways. The opening scenes of Job's story offer an image of God that everybody would like to have. He is a God who is unwaveringly in Job's corner. When the *sons of God*, God's heavenly attendants, show up to confer with the creator, God cannot stop praising Job. In fact, the particular member of the heavenly court to which he speaks is the one called *the satan*, or *the accuser*. After God learns that the satan has been going *to and fro* on the earth, God brings up the question of Job. And God repeats what the reader already knows:

> *There is no one like him on the earth, a blameless and upright man who fears God and turns away from evil.* (1:8)

What a cheerleader for Job! Who would not want to have a heavenly deity on one's side like that amidst the heavenly council? In fact, most of us wouldn't mind simply having a friend or family member who stood up for us like that, recognizing all of the good things we do, and sharing them with those who might be interested. Of course the satan is interested in Job for reasons that are not necessarily evil. We really do not want to confuse this character with the character Satan who appears later in the Bible (even though many of our English translations call him Satan and risk identifying him with the New Testament *Devil*). It's the satan's *job*, in fact, to stand against humans as their accuser before God. And that's what this character does; he entices God to take a more scrutinizing look at Job's motives.

The satan wants God to consider the possibility that Job doesn't really love God singularly, but is simply taking advantage of God's goodness (and, perhaps, God's naïveté). You might react to this complication by thinking: *Don't do it; don't let him fool you.* And in the end, this exchange between God and the satan is ultimately the explanation for Job's suffering. Job is really innocent of the whole affair.

Now we might pause and think both about the importance of our sacred stories and their costs. Having a heavenly council with a caring deity as an explanation for the way our lives turn out can be wonderfully helpful. We may not understand the decisions handed down by this council, or in Job's case, by God, who heads up the council. But that there might be such decision-making going on about our lives might in and of itself help us religious folk make more meaningful choices. That's especially so when things are going our way and God's decisions favor a pleasant life. What is more, we prefer the convenience of saying *it's God's will* rather than reflecting upon the reasons backing our moral choices. Having a God at least makes moral choices initially more convenient. And we all know that convenience is not the best reason for choosing anything. The ordinary rules of cause and effect can be suspended, we could argue, because God and his courtiers can intervene in our lives whenever it suits them.

The only problem is when God's decision-making does not go our way. Then our sacred stories get in the way. I mean, we'd all like for our gods to get things right all the time. But sometimes they do not. Or, worse, he's a God who can be enticed by such characters as his satan, and subject his loyal human subjects to all kinds of miserable pain. At such times, don't we think it might just be easier not to have anything to do with such a God? I do wonder when I get to Job's words to his wife, *Shall we receive good at the hand of God and not also receive the bad?* (2:10), if he really believes the words he's actually saying, because he finally comes around and wishes he'd never been born (3:11-16). Job's sacred story, along with his suffering, is so problematic to him when he offers those words, he'd rather not even be alive. If sacred stories can be so good to us and so bad to us at the same time, how do we decide how to live with them?

FRANK

I do not feel obliged to believe that the same God who has endowed us with sense, reason, and intellect has intended us to forgo their use.

GALILEO GALILEI

Frank is, by all appearances, a broken man. Fifteen years of marriage to an emotionally abusive woman has decimated his spirit.

"And now I'm simply trapped," he murmurs.

"Trapped?" I ask.

"Of course. The Bible says that divorce is a sin. I can either stay in my marriage, or I can leave God's will."

"Where did you get the idea God operates like that?"

Frank looks at me skeptically. "That's what the Bible says. That's what my preacher preaches."

"Frank, I don't have the right to tell anyone that his reading of the Bible may not be quite accurate, and it would be irresponsible for me to suggest you not trust your pastor. I would only say that when I read the stories of how Jesus dealt with people in pain, he seems a lot more interested in how folks experience the grace and love of God than how well they keep the rules."

There's much more to this story, but enough here for reflection. Frank has what we therapists call *boundary issues*. In some relationships, he doesn't know how to protect himself. Like a timid homeowner, he allows his wife to regularly storm into his soul and vandalize his heart while he sits helplessly. He would never allow an actual vandal to destroy his family's home. Yet he allows his wife to destroy his soul, hardly raising an objection. And he uses his religion to justify his choices. He experiences himself as trapped—as a victim.

Why are we enticed toward a God who cares little how much we suffer so long as we are keeping the rules? I suspect it is the same impulse that vaults a harsh military general to power by people who are frightened and find comfort in his brutal strength. Perhaps the safety seems worth it, until he sends his goons to conscript the boys into the army.

So, Frank has boundary issues with his wife, and with his God or, more accurately, with his religion. He allows his wife to say all manner of demeaning words to him, and he assumes he has no choice but to endure it. He allows his religion to assert all sorts of rules on his life, and he assumes he has no choice but to accept them.

"Frank, if your son made the common mistake of marrying a woman while he was too young and stupid to understand what he was getting himself into, and if the woman he married treated him like your wife treats you, what would you say to him?"

Frank's eyes tear. "I'd tell him that I love him, I'll support him in whatever be decides to do, and I'll help him as best I can."

"And you would also tell him that if he decides to leave his marriage, you wouldn't be willing to have a close and loving relationship with him anymore?"

"Of course not." Frank looks at me like I'm an alien. "I'd be there with him through thick and thin as long as he wanted my help."

"Of course you would." I insist, with my hands reaching toward the sky. "So why do you suppose you've come to believe that God wouldn't love you in the same way? I recall Jesus saying that even *pagans* know how to meet the needs of their children, and that God loves us in infinitely deeper ways."

"I never really thought about it like that before."

"Frank, you've got me curious. I'm wondering how much of your suffering is due to your marriage, and how much of it is due to your religion, or least to what your religion has taught you God expects."

REFLECTIONS

See how our expectations can create fog? We have expectations of God. We believe God has expectations of us. And we believe that all of these expectations are accurate, at least until the whirlwind breaks in. Furthermore, if we come to believe that *faith in God* somehow means that God will behave according to our expectations, then is it any wonder that many people reject faith in the aftermath of tragedy?

I (Wes) am very aware that this conversation can come perilously close to *God doesn't want you to feel bad, so do whatever feels good.* (Can you believe that a girl I was dating in college actually used those exact words with me?) This is exactly the sort of thinking the small self likes to grab hold of, so I find it important to set the context.

There are plenty of discussions among theologians of the following tenets of the Christian faith:

- God created us in a spirit of love and out of a desire for relationship.
- Creation became radically broken, and this brokenness affects all of us, fairly or not.
- Scripture offers wise counsel in the shape of rules and principles for redemptive living, but we cannot escape failing to live up to the expectations of scripture.
- When we break the rules, we are called upon to be honest with ourselves and others regarding those transgressions.
- God's grace and forgiveness are available to help us move beyond the break.

Even if you are willing to affirm my list, the question still remains: Is this enough to provide meaning in both the good times and the bad times?

4.

FEARING GOD FOR NOTHING AND PASSING THE TEST

JOB 1:9

Then satan answered the LORD, "Does Job fear God for nothing?"

CONNECTIONS

Why is knowledge so important to a meaningful life? What is it about the absence of an explanation that is so unsettling? Perhaps this is an expression of our small-self-survival instincts. If something painful happens, we want to understand *why* in order to avoid the pain the next time around. But how are we to handle circumstances for which no

21

explanation is obvious? No wonder we gravitate toward the idea that God is testing us.

The idea of God's testing his servants is fairly common among persons of faith. It is implied in the book of Job, but it is made explicit in the Jewish Talmud's (Jewish scripture) reading of both Job's story and Abraham's story. The conversation below with Mark, a Christian pastor, explores the anxiety and anger that arises as he tries to pass the test of his calling.

The Homily

Christians could benefit by knowing a bit more about the tradition of Jewish biblical interpretation, especially when it comes to Job. In the Jewish Talmud, a massive collection of ancient Jewish writings on scripture, Job's story is important in interpreting Abraham's story of his near sacrifice of Isaac (Genesis 22:1-19). A heavenly scene similar to the story of Job is used to set up a conversation between God and the satan about Abraham's righteousness. Perhaps you can imagine what comes next.

When the LORD asks how the children of earth are doing, the satan says that they are faring well. He continues by accusing humans of forsaking the LORD after they get rich from his blessings. He then calls attention to an instance in Abraham's life where a poor man went to Abraham's door to obtain food and was turned away. And there we have the ancient Jewish rabbis' explanation for why God tested Abraham by commanding him to offer his only begotten son as a sacrifice. What fascinates me is that the Talmudists were so intrigued with these two stories of Abraham and Job that they wove them together. By doing so they required interpreters to tease out the moral implications of such a retelling. The most obvious connection is that *God tested both Job and Abraham*, even though the word *test* is not used in the story of Job as it is in the story of Abraham and Isaac (see Genesis 22:1).

Pausing to reflect, I do wonder whether Christians use the idea of a *test* as a means of thinking about their own moral behavior. *I live the life I do,* one may think, *in order to pass God's test*. It's like running the race of being faithful, or of holding to the truth in the face of detractors, or of performing the proper moral action. One always wants to pass the test.

My undergraduate American Literature professor loved Hemingway. He frequently talked about Hemingway's *Death in the Afternoon* and the author's elevation of bullfighting as the symbol of the struggle of human life. Ultimately, living is an attempt to *look good in the bullring* of our lives, my instructor would say. In the bullring, fear and courage are defined, and so it is in day-to-day existence. And at that impressionable time of my life, I thought how easily this could apply to one's faith.

I wondered whether Jesus himself had *looked good in the bullring* as he stared down the challenges of his death. One of the Roman soldiers in Hemingway's short play *Today is Friday* (1926) certainly kept saying he did. And so, when I read the play, I began to question whether the metaphor really worked for Christians. That is, what would it mean to *look good in there*, for Jesus? To throw in the towel and let others kill you? No resistance at all? I mean, Jesus' clever rejoinders to his opponents only got him so far. His insistence on loving one's enemies and not resisting an evildoer (Matthew 5:28-48) are helpful in interpersonal relationships, but are they convictions that can be employed when one is staring down a government official who has the power to take your life? Can the ethos of love itself really pass the breadth of the applicability test? Well, of course, it depends upon what the aim of love is. If the aim of love is for one's own benefit, then, of course, it cannot really change much.

And that's where the book of Job comes in. The test in Job concerns a person's motives for loving God and one's neighbor. The whole test of Job is whether his or any person's moral behavior should be offered to God with no expectation of a personal benefit. I wonder if the poet himself raised this question because he had seen that quite often justice fails. Maybe he saw how people are then thrown back upon the need for patience. Patience, of course, delays the expectation, but eventually time expires on it, too.

I wonder whether the poet of Job was not wracking his brains to come up with some other basis for serving God besides justice. And on this question, Jesus *looks good* in there. For, at least as Jesus defines love of God and humans in his life and death, one does not have the expectation of a just return. In effect Jesus is also a response to the

23

satan's question of whether a person can serve God *for nothing*. The question is whether religious faith is as meaningful to us if we do it for nothing.

MARK

One of the hardest jobs in ministry is keeping your own relationship with God where it needs to be.

HAROLD WARNER

"The guy is a manipulative jerk. I can't believe anyone listens to him, yet he seems to draw people in."

I love working with pastors, though I must admit they often present a unique challenge. Whereas most of my clients are struggling with the relevance of their religious practices, most pastors I work with are in some despair over the expectations of their congregations. Mark is one such pastor. However, he is also one of the few pastors who listened when his seminary professor encouraged the class to maintain a relationship with a counselor or mentor. He comes in every few weeks.

"Is this the same guy you first brought up last summer? The retired three-star general?" I ask.

"Yeah, that's the guy. Since he can't just order people around, now he's relying on whatever he learned about being a spy. This isn't what I signed on for."

"When you responded to God's glorious *call to ministry*?"

"Yeah. Right."

"What do you suppose you *did* sign on for?"

Mark pauses and looks out the window, as though he's trying to reclaim a foggy memory. "That's a good question. I'd like to tell myself my only desire was to serve God."

"You're not sure that's the case?"

"The other evening, I was talking to my wife about my years in the insurance business. I was good at it. Sure, I had to be a salesman, but I believed that what I was selling mattered. A few years ago, I met a guy on the golf course who told me he'd always thought life insurance was a waste of money until he had kids. I asked him how much insurance he had, and he wasn't sure. A few days later he called. When he told me how much coverage he had, I pointed out that it wasn't enough to see his wife and kids through much more than a year if something happened to him. He bought a policy from me; and I'll be if he didn't die in a car wreck six months later. I still get a card from his wife every Christmas."

"Wow."

"That's what I traded for the unique opportunity of being a pastor." Mark waves his hand as though he is brushing clutter off a table.

"I know I've said this to you before, but you sure do seem angry that people end up acting like people."

"Do they have to act so much like people all of the time?" He's now gazing out that window that seems so popular. His voice has dropped to a whisper.

"Oh, come on. What about that sweet old lady who brings you a flower from her garden every Sunday so you can look classy in the pulpit?"

Mark turns back to me, with a hint of a smile. "She is a sweet old lady. And a lonely old lady," he admits. "I should probably get by to see her at home more often."

"I'm thinking about Wendell Berry's comparison of pastoring to farming. I think it's in his book of essays, *Standing by Words*. Anyway, Berry says that when a man is buying a farm, he has all these ideas about what he is going to do with the farm. Once he starts working, he discovers what the farm will let him do. It's not the farm's fault the place he wanted to put up a barn is solid rock under six inches of soil."

"OK, I get your point…I think."

"It seems to me that you are dealing with a classic small self/ Authentic Self struggle here. Your Authentic Self really does embrace lofty goals, but your small self still wants some sort of pay-off. Is your small self angry that the farm won't cooperate?"

"Why shouldn't I be angry when church members act like underhanded politicians?"

"I suppose there's some room for righteous indignation. I'm just wondering if your small self is working you even more than that general does. Success in the insurance business is all about building relationships, isn't it? Are you surprised that ministry is the same?"

"In insurance I could just move on from people who didn't value what I was selling."

"That's an important difference. Maybe you've bought a farm that is pushing you to up your farming skills. What if God has called you to a farm that someone else is going to harvest? Could you live with that?"

"I hate it when you say stuff like that." I think he's kidding, but I'm not entirely sure....

"Yeah." I lean in, "That's why I get paid the big bucks...to annoy people."

REFLECTIONS

There's just no getting away from the notion of expectations. This pastor, like most, responds to a desire to serve others without a conscious expectation of payoff. Yet, how else are we to explain his frustration? Being a pastor is proving much more complicated than he expected.

Furthermore, Mark's experience raises questions for all of us about what relationships require of us. When we hear him being so deadly earnest and honest about his feelings for one of his congregants, we do wonder how such honesty could ever live in the world beyond the counseling session. It's one thing for Mark to talk to his therapist about such things, but does he have an *obligation* to *speak truth in love* to the retired general? What do you consider your obligation to be when it comes to conflict?

The story of Job wants to peel back the layers and peer beneath the surface to encounter Job's feelings about God. But it's also about whether those motives must be pure in order for persons like Mark to be effective as a minister. The notion of *kavanah* in Judaism is variously interpreted, but it refers generally to the proper attitude one has as one fulfills the commandments. Without the proper attitude, the commandment remains unfulfilled. We all know that Mark probably could fulfill his pastoral duties by simply doing the right things even though he was not doing them with the right attitude.

5

FEARING GOD TOO MUCH

JOB 1:9-10

Have you not put a fence around him and his house and all that he has, on every side? You have blessed the work of his hands, and his possessions have increased in the land.

CONNECTIONS

Do you love God simply because, as many catchy worship choruses proclaim, God is worthy of love, praise, and adoration for no other reason than, well, God is God?

The phrase *fearing God for nothing* may seem puzzling to us. Another way to understand the satan's questioning of Job's devotion would be, *Does Job love God simply because he loves God, or does he love God because he gets something out of the deal?* Our observation is that many people believe they are loving God without strings attached, only to discover they've had more expectations than they realized when the whirlwind hits.

However, another implication of Job's fearing God *for nothing* is that in times of trouble he's just supposed to sit there and endure it as though such trouble is a part of fearing God. In the counseling session it sounds as though James has received similar counsel in his time of grief, and he's sick of it.

THE HOMILY

Does Job know he fears God for nothing? Although there is no way to know for sure, we contemporary readers might imagine that Ecclesiastes' enigmatic bit of counsel in 7:16-17 has something to do with biblical characters like Job. *Do not be too righteous, and do not act too wise; why should you destroy yourself? Do not be too wicked, and do not be a fool; why should you die before your time?* It seems to be a frank assertion that it is possible to be too righteous and that such behavior, just like being overly wicked, leads to self-destruction. The implication may be that the art of living is holding these two forces in some kind of healthy relationship.

In a more artistic way, the poet of Job is raising the same question: Is fearing God for nothing too costly a thing? When the satan asks God whether Job *fears God for nothing*, his words may be jarring. He suggests that the highest virtue is the kind that offers trust with no expectation of any sort of return. But the poet, by putting these words on the satan's lips, may be questioning the principle. Clearly, God thinks Job is a righteous man. Commentators note that he is not sinless, but that he is blameless (1:1, 8). But God offers nothing by way of definition as to the terms of that righteousness. We are left to wonder whether one's motives for virtuous behavior are actually important. Ancient thinkers did the same: *All one's ways may be pure in one's own eyes, but the LORD weighs the spirit* (Proverbs 16:3).

Is it enough to feed the poor and provide homes for the homeless, or is such action somehow diminished if one does it, say, as a business in order to make a profit? Or, say, as a congregation of believers in order to provide some reason for existence? *What's the harm in benefitting from good deeds?* we might ask. The good is still done, right? People who are in need of such provision are experiencing the satisfaction of those needs, right? So, why should God only be pleased with virtuous actions that bring no benefit to the one who performs such action?

Are there really religious people who are totally selfless? I cannot remember when the sermons I've heard have ever insisted on such a thing. Of course, Jesus' story in the Gospels is a pretty good example of a selfless death in that they claim he offers no resistance to his persecutors. On the other hand, the more we Christians elevate Jesus' status to that of the all-knowing Christ—who had the motive of saving the world, knowing in advance how all things would turn out—detracts from the judgment of selflessness, doesn't it? So, are there other examples we might appeal to in order to determine if such selflessness is required of virtuous action?

What about Abraham? Perhaps his near offering of Isaac as a sacrifice should be considered a selfless act (Genesis 22:1-19). It is surprising that the Abraham who protests against God's destruction of Sodom and Gomorrah (Genesis 18:25) remains silent at the injustice when it involves his only son. On the other hand, the satan might dispel our sympathetic notions by saying *Skin for skin! All that people have they will give to save their lives* (2:4). Well, what about the three young men (Hananiah, Mishael, and Azariah—Shadrach, Meshach, and Abednego) thrown into Nebuchadnezzar's furnace for not worshiping the king's gods? Their words to the king are:

> *If our God whom we serve is able to deliver us from the furnace of blazing fire and out of your hand, O king, let him deliver us. But if not, be it known to you, O king, that we will not serve your gods...* (Daniel 3:17-18)

The three young men certainly seem selfless.

But who performs the virtuous behaviors of religious faith so selflessly? And where is it a requirement that one do so? In the end, don't people of faith hold on to faith for a good reason: because it makes life meaningful by providing a purpose? A sense of spirituality, or of God's presence, calms the over-active mind. It allows us to let go and find peace. Isn't that why we join together as a people of religious faith?

Even so, it seems to me that it would be difficult to argue that this is really selfless.

JAMES

Holding on to anger is like grasping a hot coal with the intent of throwing it at someone else; you are the one who gets burned.

THE BUDDHA

James is so angry. And he has been angry for four years. He was sixteen years old when his big sister was killed in a freak car accident. He still recalls the well-meaning people making silly comments at the funeral about God's will and how wonderful heaven is.

"What hypocrites," James hisses. "They're just glad it was our family and not theirs."

We've been over this ground more than a few times since James started seeing me four months ago. And we'll return to this ground as often as he needs to. A handsome college student, James *gave his heart to Jesus* when he was eight years old. His mother prayed with him that evening many years ago, and he's watched her turn into a ghost since the death of her child. He is a bright young man, barely maintaining a B average, and making good use of the available alcohol and pot on campus in order to get through the day.

His tuition is covered by the insurance settlement from the accident.

Our first appointment was memorable. He told me about his sister's death. When finished, he leaned forward and then offered these jarring words:

"Don't fucking tell me to get over it."

"Nobody has a right to tell you to get over anything," was the only honest response I could muster.

On this day, four months later, I decide to take a risk, hoping I've not misjudged the strength of our connection.

"James, would you try again to help me better understand your anger?"

James rolls his eyes. "My sister was killed in a senseless accident, and my family has been falling apart ever since. Isn't that enough?"

"Of course it's enough, but I still want to grasp this better. It is as though you are declaring that your life can't possibly be 'OK' ever again. Please hang in with me here. I know that what I'm saying could seem offensive to some, but I'm truly just trying to know you more deeply. I'm wondering how much of your pain is about the real grief of losing someone you love, and how much of it is about your sense of injustice."

"Well, it's sure as hell not fair." The fire has faded.

"No, it's not fair. Yet, you're a bright guy who has been aware of all the crap that happens in the world since you were old enough to read a newspaper. You've known for a long time that, whatever God's intentions, God obviously doesn't step in to make life fair."

"Then what's the point? What's the point in even believing in God?"

Now it's my turn to gaze out the window. "Believe me, I ask myself that question on a regular basis. But all I know is to return to what my religious tradition teaches. God is redeeming a broken creation, and our investment in life allows us to partner with God in that redemption."

"My Sunday school teachers never said anything like that."

"I'm not surprised, and it always saddens me when I'm reminded how poorly most religious education prepares us for real life. I know our Sunday school experiences are separated by forty years, but I suspect the lessons were the same. I was led to believe that if I played the game by the rules, God would reward me with certain blessings and protection."

"Yep, that's the same shit I got."

"Why do you suppose that is?" I feel very much like a fellow struggler, asking the same impossible questions as James. "I mean, you know that at least a few of our teachers had been through awful things. I wonder why they just kept dishing out the same dishonest drivel?"

James is quiet for a moment. "I think I was in the third grade when my Sunday school teacher had a miscarriage. She had been so excited she was pregnant, and we boys thought it was cool that she would tell us how it felt to have a baby growing inside of her…how tired she was… and how she kept sending her husband to the store for weird snacks. Then it was just over. She was not there one Sunday. The other teacher told us that she'd lost the baby. Then she added that it must not have been God's will for our teacher to have that baby. I don't recall even seeing her at church again."

"James...how confusing that must have been for you, and to me. That's just what I'm talking about. Real life breaks in. A kid needs to know how to make sense of it. The adults just shrink back and leave us to figure things out some other way. Is it any wonder that so many people simply find religion irrelevant?"

"Maybe it is," He offers softly.

"Maybe. But, please, don't confuse dishonest religion with being a follower."

REFLECTIONS

Milton: I'm not sure the distinction between *dishonest religion* and *follower* still gets at what we're intending. The term *follower* might just mean that James is participating in an unhealthy kind of religious faith.

Wes: Well, I'm not crazy about using the term *religion*, anyway. By *dishonest religion* I'm trying to clarify the way I think that some (many?) people hold to and practice religion. By *follower* I'm distinguishing between those who actually practice this kind of honest religion and those who do not.

Milton: Yes, but such dichotomies often are simply ways of saying, *You or your practice is different than mine, and therefore you must be wrong.* Practitioners of any religion distinguish between their own points of view and that of anyone who happens to differ with them.

Wes: Well, I'm not saying that, here, though, I don't think. Talk more about what you're seeing.

Milton: OK. One of the older articles I have my students read is about comparative religion.[4] The author argues that all religion has both an objective and a subjective aspect to it. The objective aspect we might think of as tradition. The subjective we might call faith. Both are essential to defining what we mean when we study religion. So, you

---

[4] Antonio R. Gualtieri, "What Is Comparative Religion Comparing? The Subject Matter of Religious Studies," *Journal for the Scientific Study of Religion* (June 1, 1967): 31–34.

cannot condemn one and embrace the other, which is what it sounds like you're doing there with James.

Wes: I don't disagree with that, generally, Milton. But I think James needs to explore more carefully his own understanding of the subjective aspects of his religious tradition. That's where the distinction between small self versus Authentic Self may be helpful. In his practice of what you call the subjective side of religion, he is allowing his small-self emotions to determine his understanding of religious faith. By using the word *follower*, I am getting at his need to understand his Authentic Self, and how his small-self emotions can be developed and transformed into much healthier feelings about the tradition in which he was raised.

Milton: I get it. I guess most of your clients are seeing you because their understanding of religious faith hasn't really helped them sort out their own emotional complexities.

Wes: Yeah. I'm reminded of Richard Rohr's distinction between the *container* and the *Contained*. God cannot be completely grasped by any religious system, but healthy religion helps us build a container that holds a portion of the mystery, and offers us some initial ways of working out our questions. Rohr further points out how tempting it is to simply equate the container with God. There can be great comfort in deciding that *my* religion is *the* religion. At least until life breaks in with a fury.

6

Holding Convictions Because of Blessing

Job 1:10

You have blessed the work of his hands…

Connections

Please take a moment and ask yourself: *Do I love God simply because God is worthy of my love?* If you answered *yes*, then how do you know?

Again, we consider the satan's contention that Job's moral action is only motivated by his expectation of God's blessing. This dilemma is central to the concepts of small self and Authentic Self we have introduced. As you read, keep in mind that the Authentic Self desires to be present to God with no agenda. The small self is always looking for an angle, keeping an eye out for the pay-off.

Notice what you think and feel as the homily challenges our commonly held assumptions about God's justice. As you read the counseling session, ask yourself if you have anything in common with Dan's expectations, and his anger.

THE HOMILY

So many ideas and experiences filter into our motives for our choices. When we come to the book of Job, we are expected to consider the proposition that God governs human destiny justly. Or, if it's not God, then there is some principle at work in the universe that does so. When we talk about a *moral order* of the universe, we mean something like that which Martin Luther King Jr. meant when he borrowed the phrase, *the arc of the moral universe is long, but it bends toward justice.* We cannot tell what the satan believes about the moral order of the universe. Nevertheless, it seems that his accusation of God goes one of two ways:

1. Either God has misled Job (by *blessing the work of his hands*) into *thinking* that the universe is governed by some principal of moral justice; or
2. The satan himself actually believes that God maintains such an order of the universe.

If the satan's statements are founded on the former view, he is indicting God. If the latter, he is indicting Job. But serving God *for nothing*, or selflessly, would make the actual order of the universe irrelevant, it would seem. At least this is what the satan wants to find out about Job: Is Job's own benefit his motivation for service to God? *Blessing*, of course, is often just religious talk for *things are going well with me.* And, of course, for persons who believe there is a rather strict moral order in the universe, blessing means that, first, they have been performing up to God's expected moral standards, and second, their blessing is their reward. They deserve it, in other words, given the presumed terms of God's governance of the universe.

And likewise, when people are being treated unjustly and abusively, appealing to some principal of order, or a "moral arc of the universe," is a way of encouraging people to continue on in their cause. It's like those marchers who joined Martin Luther King Jr. on that walk from Selma to Montgomery in March of 1965 and were stopped and beaten at the Edmund Pettus Bridge. King's words to them invoked his firm belief in a morally ordered universe. His intent was, among other things, to get his followers to keep trying…to not give up. He was relying upon their assumption that, despite all appearances, the universe is governed by a just God who won't let evil finally prevail. And there is the rub. For people who are suffering the worst kinds of injustices in the world, the religious response is often one of convincing them that ultimately all injustices will be set right.

In a broader sense, it *is* religion's task to make good sense of those experiences that are unjust. And pressing the argument for a just culmination for all things leaves the rather long and arduous waiting period called life. For religious folk, this may not only mean holding fast to their commitments, but witnessing a lot of pain and suffering on the part of others, too.

How many MLK birthday celebrations have you been to? And how many times have you heard some White Anglo-Saxon Protestant dignitary pontificating about how much better things are for people of color on the home front? Are white people really the ones to ask? I'm sure I have wondered with many others whether MLK, if he were to return to this life, would still believe that there is a moral arc of the universe. Would he agree with white people that things have really gotten that much better in the United States for black people? Arguing *for* a justly governed universe may actually increase injustice rather than decrease it. We become so convinced by our rhetoric that we fail to see the injustices that actually exist.

The sage who observed that the counsel in a person's heart is like deep water (Proverbs 20:5) must surely have known the difficulty of trying to bring to light another person's most inner thoughts. He adds that it takes good sense to draw it out. It's not necessarily clear what Job himself believes about a justly governed universe. There's no question he worries about whether his children might have offended God somehow, either by their partying or by their improper attempts to offer satisfaction afterward (1:5). This would favor a view that Job really believes in a morally ordered universe. Neither is there any doubt in our minds that Job himself is a virtuous man, taking his own moral behavior very seriously. But if Job's motives for his goodness grow from his blessed life and his belief in a justly governed universe, then we, like the satan, want to see how he deals with life when those principles are crushed.

DAN

In all affairs it's a healthy thing now and then to hang a question mark on the things you have long taken for granted.

BERTRAND RUSSELL

"And don't say, 'At least you didn't wake up in Haiti.'"

For the record, I've never actually said this to Dan. I think during our second conversation I shared my *go-to* phrase when I sense my small self stirring up discontent. *At least I didn't wake up in Haiti* is my way of reframing discontent when I feel my anxiety creeping up. I've told Dan that I struggle with a bit of an anxiety disorder myself, though I haven't told him about *The Great Darkness of '97* that turned me into a dysfunctional mess for nearly two years.

"You know, Dan, I've never said that to you. I only say it to myself. But what is it about that phrase that gets under your skin?"

"It's so dismissive. It reminds me of my mother telling me that the starving children in China would be glad to eat my broccoli."

"Isn't it interesting how even kids seem to know when they are being manipulated with truth?"

"What the hell is that supposed to mean?"

"Well, isn't it true that there *are* hungry children all around the world who would be glad to eat the food that spoiled children don't want?"

"I suppose." Now Dan is at least looking curious.

"So your mom was telling the truth, but even as a kid you knew you were being manipulated. I get accused of the same thing all the time. You know, it's just not fair that I get thrown under the bus because of all those moms who are worried about their kids' eating habits."

"That's a joke, right?"

I laugh. "Only sort of. Tell me if I've got this straight. When your father died ten years ago, he left your drug-addicted sister twice as much money in the will as he left you. Your mom defends dad's decisions by explaining your sister just has more problems than you. Since then your sister has snorted most of what dad left her up her nose, and now your mom is taking care of her, despite the fact that her own health problems are mounting."

"That's a decent summary."

"Also, you've joined and left three different churches because each pastor offered you the same trite *wisdom* about how you didn't need to concern yourself with God's way of doling out justice."

"That's true."

"And you are now here talking to me because your cardiologist almost threatened to drop you as a patient if you didn't get some help for your anger."

"Again, accurate."

"One last thing. You've built a successful business, are married to a wonderful woman, and have two great kids. However, your wife's patience is beginning to run out. She's tired of the church hopping, and you are wondering if she might actually leave."

Suddenly it looks like all of the air has gone out of Dan's balloon. "Man, when you lay it out like that, I sound like a real jerk."

"It's actually my conviction that you are *not* a jerk that has me so curious. I'm reminded of what I recently heard a comedian say, *My life is great, but my perception sucks.* The stuff with your mom and sister is genuinely painful, yet wouldn't most of your friends say that the good things in your life far outweigh the pain?"

"Well, when you put it so directly, I'm not sure my friends would say that. In fact, since you brought up my friends, I'm trying to think how I would have a serious conversation like we're having with any one of them."

"Have you tried?"

"Hell, no. Well, maybe that's not entirely true. I've been playing golf every Thursday morning with the same three guys for years. I've mentioned some of this on the course from time to time. And I'm recalling that I sort of freaked them all out on the first tee a few months ago."

"Yeah?"

"I think I'd been on the phone with my mom that morning, listening to her drone on about my sister…again. I was a little late for golf, and when I walked up to the guys, I said something like, *Hey, if the police ever find my sister floating in the river, you guys will cover for me won't you?* They didn't seem to realize I was joking."

"I can see where you might have caught them off guard just a bit."

Dan laughs. "Yeah. They stared at me for a moment, and then someone blurted out, *So…who goes first?*"

"Testosterone poisoning."

"What?"

"You know…testosterone. It messes with the male brain, so we're terrified of dealing with emotion. Women don't seem to have the same problem. It can leave us guys feeling very isolated in our struggles. My guess is your friends, like your wife, can't understand why you won't just let this go. When you were describing the scene on the golf course, a picture of an actor suddenly popped into my mind."

"An actor?"

"Yeah. Bruce Willis, of all people. It occurs to me that you seem like one of those Bruce Willis characters. You know, when he plays some guy who is determined to root out an injustice, and seems to alienate everyone in his life along the way?"

"OK. Maybe that fits… a little…"

"But here's what's got me baffled. In those movies, it's always clear what the injustice is about. The writers always make sure that we, the audience, understand clearly what Bruce is so torqued out about, and why he must put things right. He comes off as heroic in his willingness to lose everything in the name of justice. With you, I can't figure out exactly what you are fighting for in the name of justice. If you were to win this battle, who would be cheering?"

Dan seems focused on that little stain on the carpet. After a few moments he offers, "My dad?"

"Your dad?"

"I never thought about it like this before, but maybe I'm fighting for my dad."

"How so?"

"Well, he did work his ass off to make a living. He made a lot more than a living, he made sure our family had all the things he didn't have growing up. And when my sister started screwing up, the tension between him and my mom mounted. He tried to hold sis accountable, but, to me, it always looked like mom was going behind his back and rescuing her."

"That had to be hard to watch."

"Yeah. Our family sort of divided down the middle. Me and dad on one side, mom and sis on the other. It's not like things were bad for me. I got tons of attention from him. Lots of golf and fishing. Lots of Dubl-R burgers on Saturday afternoons." Dan's eyes start to fill with tears.

"What great memories. But he ended up leaving your sister a lot more in the will?"

"The lawyer said that the last change to his will occurred about two months before he died. He'd been under hospice care for about month at that point. The nurse was a godsend as far as managing dad's pain was concerned, but it meant he wasn't always in his right mind."

"And you're wondering if your mom *negotiated* a change in his will during that time?"

"Yeah."

"You can't prove it, and there's not a damned thing you could do about it if you could."

"Yeah."

"Man, suddenly I feel like rooting for you, only the writers of your movie haven't left you with any way to win. That is, unless you are willing to consider peacefully moving forward with your life as a form of winning."

"Yeah." With each "yeah" I see the fire returning to Dan's eyes.

"One question before we wrap up this conversation. We'll pick up here next time. Would your dad want you to ruin your life over your outrage on his behalf?"

REFLECTIONS

No one doubts that one way people respond to injustice is through anger. Anger eventually finds expressions in all sorts of ways. It could lead to violence, too. The reference to MLK evokes the memory that he counseled the avoidance of violence. I (Milton) do wonder whether his followers really believed that eventually justice would prevail or whether they just loved him.

The homily seeks to raise the difficulty of really knowing what lies buried within a person's deepest thoughts; the wisdom the counselor shows is in the ability to surface what lies deeply buried inside Dan's emotional history.

The counseling session with Dan also provokes a recollection of Jesus' counsel to a man who sought him *to tell my brother to divide the family inheritance with me* (Luke 12:13). Jesus sidesteps the request, urging that he is not the judge of such things. The incident becomes the basis for Luke's admonition about the dangers of greed (Luke 12:15-21). The parable that follows the instruction concerns the prosperity of a farmer who has to build bigger barns to store the abundance of his crops. The context, though, aims to suggest that material wealth does not matter much in cases where one is called upon by God to give an account for one's soul.

Why couldn't we read the parable in Luke as an example of God's blessing, though? On the other hand, why would God bless a person so abundantly only to demand his soul on the very night of his triumph? Is that just?

7.

CURSE GOD AND DIE

JOB 2:9

Then his wife said to him, Do you still persist in your integrity? Curse God, and die.

CONNECTIONS

What do you think of Job's wife? Are you irritated with her insensitivity? Are you annoyed that Job doesn't even seem to notice her until she speaks? Job's wife has also lost everything. The only element of God's game that has been spared her are the painful boils, yet she is relegated to a bit part in the drama. The original readers/hearers of this story might hardly have noticed, since they would have considered a wife little more than the property of the husband.

Yet, it is worth noting that Job's wife is telling the absolute truth about the implications of Job's stance. How do you react to her words? Does she seem like an uncompassionate shrew? Or do you find her simply honest? And what does it look like when we place the relational stress of a husband's crisis within a modern context?

THE HOMILY

Which irritates you more with Job's story: that Job's wife seems so insensitive or that it takes the poet so long before he even considers her? She finally speaks, though, and says, *bless God and die*. That's right. The Hebrew text is *barek*, the imperative for *bless*, not *curse*.

Many of you have been taught that the text reflects the substitution of the word *bless* for the word *curse*. Most scholars assume that later editors of the text made the substitution because they considered it almost blasphemous to even write the phrase *curse God*. Reading the text as it stands, though, with the word *bless*, would make Job's subsequent response significant in another way. It would not be the *blessing* for which he would be accusing his wife of folly, but quite possibly the *dying* part; as if to ask his wife, Why would *blessing* God lead to my death? But of course, we know that central to the terms of the story is Job's pious naïveté, which leads to his lamentable situation in the first place.

Despite the fact that Job's wife only opens her mouth to her husband after the passage of time, she is there throughout the story. Did you notice her? She is there as early as the first reference to Job's ten children (1:2). For how else could those children even be Job's without his lifelong partner? She is there when the servants of the house are mentioned, because who else would supervise the household (1:3)? She is present when the satan says to God, But stretch out your hand now, and touch all that he has… (1:11), for in the ancient world, Job's wife would have been counted among his possessions. And likewise she's there when that fourth messenger comes and says your sons and daughters were eating and drinking wine in their eldest brothers house… (1:18), because these are her children, too.

If the first time you notice Job's wife is when she speaks, you may be like so many others who embrace the patriarchal nature of the biblical story. The woman's point of view of the disaster she shares is offered almost as an aside.

Does Job's wife share the same moral convictions? Would Job's wife have been considered blameless and upright also? Does this even matter? The satan's test is about whether Job *fears God for nothing*, not whether his wife does. Perhaps for the writer of this book, she is intended as only a prop in a fable. But we modern readers, hopefully, cannot dismiss her so easily.

Let us remember that she is as ignorant of the heavenly test as is Job. And for all she knows, her horrible situation is her husband's own fault. What must be going through her mind? Her husband is sitting there, ruminating about his moral principles, when there are other very pressing and practical issues to be considered. Her jarring words, *bless God and die*, call our attention to a vast incongruity. Job is preoccupied with his own moral virtue while his wife is left alone with her own suffering.

Maybe the words of Job's wife call us to think beyond the story in ways the original readers might never have done. Job's wife is truly an innocent bystander caught in the collateral damage of Job's moral convictions.

JEANINE

And despite the fact that Job's wife only opens her mouth to her husband after the passage of time, she is there throughout the story.

MILTON HORNE

"Thanks for coming in, Jeanine. There are some circumstances I know I'll never fully understand unless I hear from the spouse. I appreciate you taking some time from your busy day to speak with me."

In our e-mail communication to set up this session, it was clear Jeanine would be a reluctant participant. I assured her I wasn't trying to rope her into marriage counseling. Understandably, when someone like me approaches someone in Jeanine's shoes, he or she assumes that I'm going to be just one more voice admonishing, "You must stay in your marriage!"

"What I *think* I know is that Raymond has spent most of the last year in bed, leaving you to handle everything related to the home and kids. But how would you describe the situation?"

"That's a pretty good summary. His construction business went under after the tornado two years ago, and it took six months for him to figure out he was not properly insured. At least it took six months for him to tell *me* that he wasn't getting any insurance money to replace all of his equipment. He ran around like a chicken with its head cut off for a little while, and then just sort of collapsed."

"What an awful situation."

"Yep, that's what it's like to be married to Mr. Perfect after Mr. Perfect hits the skids."

"If you'll pardon me for stating the obvious, you sound angry."

Jeanine's eyes bore in on me like she's not sure I understand the obvious. "Fucking right, I'm angry. My apologies for language unbecoming a *lady*."

"No apology necessary. Raymond seems pretty sure you're done. He says that once your nursing license is back up to date, he expects you to take the kids and move back to where your parents live. I don't want you to tell me anything that you wouldn't tell Raymond, but in order to help him, I need to have an idea of what kind of support he can expect."

"I'm afraid there won't be much coming from me. When business was booming he didn't care what I thought, and now that the business has cratered he just wants me to clean up the mess while he lies in the bed and moans."

"He didn't care what you thought when things were on the upswing?"

"Nope." Her hand swats air as though she's seen a fly. The money started coming in six years ago, and I started asking him about getting the college funds up to speed. He ignored that, but didn't have any trouble dropping ten grand into the capital campaign at church."

"OK, you've got my curiosity stirring. It sounds like you were fairly sure about how the finances should have been handled. Do you know why you sat back and let things head down a dangerous road?"

"What was I supposed to do? He wouldn't listen to me."

"I'm not sure there was anything in particular you were *supposed* to do. I'm just always curious about how we sometimes remain passive when we see danger on the horizon. Maybe you can help me gain a bit more insight. For instance, if you could tell that the brakes on your car were not working right, and if Raymond would not take the time to get it fixed, would you just keep driving the car until you wrecked?"

"That actually happened."

"You wrecked?"

"No, I mean that a few years back the van started pulling hard to the right whenever I would brake. It scared the shit out of me, but Raymond wouldn't take the time to get the van to the shop."

"What finally happened?"

"One day I was driving by a mechanic's shop and thought, *I'm sick of this* and pulled into the place. The old guy was great. He took a look and was able to fix it on the spot. He told me I was lucky he had the parts on hand."

"Wow, a mechanic who fixes something on the spot? And people say miracles don't happen anymore."

Jeanine smiles. "Yeah. He told me that he'd noticed the two children's car seats, and didn't figure it was a good idea to put me on the waiting list."

"See? This is what I'm talking about. Why is it that in some situations we take action to get things done, and in others, we don't?"

"Good question" she says thoughtfully. I guess having someone look at the brakes seems a lot simpler than taking over the finances. Raymond always acted like the money side of things was his domain. But now you've got me curious too. Why didn't I take a stronger stand?"

REFLECTIONS

There's simply no way to truly wrap our modern, Western minds around the social context of Job's story. The notion that a wife would be an equal partner in marriage would have been inconceivable to original listeners of this story. We bristle at the thought of a man treating his wife like property and expecting her to quietly fulfill her duties.

Yet, how often do both husbands and wives relegate themselves to such a position?

Wes: I often hear people saying something like, "I've seen this coming for years," and yet also agreeing that they weren't willing to intervene actively enough to create change. When we do this, it's almost as though we are choosing to be "property."

Milton: I see what you mean, but I'm stuck on the progress this single counseling session appears to make, wherein Jeanine seems to transform her anger into something more helpful. Her recollection of the car-repair incident does make her wonder why she did not intervene in the family finances. But, does she feel any better?

Wes: Does she *feel* any better? I guess I see that as both a very relevant *and* very irrelevant question at the same time. There's nothing wrong with wanting to feel better, but aren't we pushing our readers to consider placing honesty about faith above the goal of feeling better?

Milton: Yes, we are asking people to consider honesty and integrity, despite whatever pain it might entail. I'm just struck, in reading the narratives, by the unintended consequences of honesty. I'm seeing how such honesty in one arena carries the potential to uncover other buried feelings about oneself. I cannot help but think that now Jeanine is blaming herself instead of her husband for their circumstances.

Wes: That's certainly a risk, Milt. Of course, this would be an example of how clever the small self can be in shifting focus. To move from, "My husband's a loser" to "I'm a loser" is a small-self lateral move at best. Hopefully the woman in this story will seek help in unpacking the choices that brought her life to where it is. Although, in this narrative, Jeanine is not my client, it's not unusual for a person to contact me, sometimes months later, and ask me to help them take a fresh look at things.

8

THEN JOB OPENED HIS MOUTH

After this Job opened his mouth and cursed the day of his birth.

CONNECTIONS

Have you ever thought you'd made peace with a situation, only to find yourself erupting at a least expected moment? The story of Job takes a jarring turn when he finally begins to reveal to his friends, and to God, what he's really feeling. This man, who previously seemed to be passively accepting his plight, suddenly erupts with vitriol towards God. His friends are shocked. We're not told whether or not God is shocked. Is God offended? Does God admire Job's honesty? Does Job's honesty threaten their relationship? Does it ever occur to God that Job might decide the relationship is not worth it?

From our contemporary perspective, we want to believe that God is more than able to receive this abuse from Job and still love him. After all, God did set him up. The setting for the pastoral conversation suggests how these dynamics often play out in relationships involving only flesh-and-blood human beings.

THE HOMILY

One dilemma facing those who carefully study the book of Job is explaining why Job suddenly begins to curse. Many of us have been instructed by that wonderful bit of advice in Proverbs 17:28:

Even fools who keep silent are considered wise; when they close their lips, they are deemed intelligent. Silence can conceal either wisdom or foolishness. If Job is indeed a wise person, shouldn't we expect him to eventually open his mouth and say something? Certainly to God, but also to his friends who had come to comfort him. But what comes out is so angry and violent that it strains our normal sense of decorum. What was he thinking? Perhaps something akin to the prophet Jeremiah's words: *O LORD, you have enticed me, and I was enticed; you have overpowered me, and you have prevailed* (Jeremiah 20:7).

Jeremiah is the only other figure in the Old or New Testaments to curse the day of his birth in helpless frustration and anger (Jeremiah 20:14). Yet later writers ignore Job's outburst. The later Christian and Islamic reflections on Job could leave a person wondering if these writers had actually read the original story. Neither mentions Job's angry curse. The New Testament mentions Job one time and only offers him as an example of patient endurance (James 5:11). In that same context, scripture also appeals to the prophets as examples of patience. Why would Christians remember the story of Job in such an abbreviated way? The Muslim tradition at least gives more references to Job. He is mentioned four times in the Qur'an (4:163; 6:84; 21:83-84; 38:44). Two times Job is mentioned in the context of other prophets given special blessings from God. Two other times he is mentioned as an example of extraordinary patience. For some reason, these later traditions did not think it important to point out Job's angry words directed toward God.

The more pressing question, though, is whether Job's words to God really threatened to break their relationship. After all, his opening words in chapter 3 put forward a curse of his *own* birth, which would seem to assume a curse of God's management of the universe. His final words in Job 31 are again in the form of a curse upon himself. His anger seems serious enough. But even the Qur'an knows God as the forgiver of sins and accepter of repentance (40:2). Could God really hold such words against Job? God surely understood that Job was suffering, and he spoke out of his honesty and integrity. Even more so, as the story reveals, God eventually acknowledges that Job was speaking in ignorance (38:1-2). So, how could Job's words possibly damage his relationship with the all-powerful creator of the universe? Especially when that creator is not only forgiving and discerning, but knows what actually goes on within the hearts of persons (Proverbs 16:2-3)?

Besides, was what Job said to God any worse than what other of God's servants said to him? There's Abraham, of course, who implicitly accuses God of injustice in the destruction of Sodom and Gomorrah: *Shall not the judge of all the earth do what is just?* (Genesis 18:25). Then there's David and his liturgical songs: *My God, my God, why have you forsaken me?* (Psalm 22:1). And Elijah, whose depression calls forth this complaint: *I have been very zealous for the LORD, the God of hosts; for the Israelites have forsaken your covenant, thrown down your altars, and killed your prophets with the sword. I alone am left, and they are seeking my life, to take it away* (1 Kings 19:10). Then, there's Jeremiah, another prophet, whose words convey the most pointed of criticisms: *Why is my pain unceasing, my wound incurable, refusing to be healed? Truly, you are to me like a deceitful brook, like waters that fail* (Jeremiah 15:18). He adds, *Correct me, O LORD, but in just measure; not in your anger, or you will bring me to nothing* (10:24).

If holding religious faith is indeed about honesty, then Job is the model. He does not seem to mince words when he finally speaks to God. And such honesty does not seem to bother God, either.

NICK

Most people want to be circled by safety, not by the unexpected.
The unexpected can take you out. But the unexpected can also
take you over and change your life. Put a heart in your body
where a stone used to be.

RON HALL

"Thank you so much for seeing me. I'm a mess. I've been up all night. I couldn't go to work like this."

"I'm just glad I had a last-minute cancellation." Nick had left me a frantic voice mail earlier that morning, and then I noticed that my noon appointment time had just opened up. I immediately recognized him from a class I'd taught at a local church a few months ago.

"She just up and left. When I got home last night, around ten, there was a note on the kitchen table that said, 'I'm done.' Her car was gone. She wouldn't answer her phone. When I finally texted that I was worried and about to call the police, she sent back, 'I'm fine.' She wouldn't tell me where she was."

"Had anything in particular happened during the day? Something she might have been upset about?"

Nick's head is buried in his hands, leaning forward, almost like he is praying. "Not that I know of. She sounded a little irritated when I called her from the bar to let her know I was having drinks with a couple of buddies. I think I called around five-thirty or six. She said something about dinner being almost ready and hung up." He looks up at me. "God, I just can't believe she'd take off like this."

"Nick, I know you are incredibly upset right now. There's usually some sort of reasonable explanation for these things. Can you think of anything else that might explain her disappearing act?"

"I thought things were great. I'd even attended that class you did on marriage stuff after she insisted. I usually hate those sorts of things. At least you were entertaining." He offers the hint of a smile. "What was that one 'crazy rule' you talked about? Something about mind-reading?"

"If you really love me, you'll read my mind."

Some things are taking shape in my mind as we talk. I'd taught my *Ten Crazy Rules of Relationships* class at their church. Nick's wife had attended every week. I think Nick showed up about week three or four. And, if I'm recalling correctly, Nick's wife stopped me after the first class and asked the all-too-common question about how to get her spouse to attend. I'm sure I answered her the way I always do. Rather than bring it up over and over and risk being dismissed as a nag, I recommend spouses frame such requests in terms of a gift. For example, she could say, "I know you don't like these sorts of things, but it would be a real gift if you would attend with me." I don't know what tactic Nick's wife took, but he started showing up.

I lean in. "Nick, I can see that you're shocked by all of this, but it is very rare for someone to suddenly change course like this with no warning whatsoever. How would you describe your marriage in general?"

"It's been great for the ten years we've been married. Sam's never had to work, and she's always made sure the house was clean and dinner was on the table. I guess it was hard for her when the doc said she couldn't have kids. And when I told her I didn't care about adoption stuff, she seemed fine with it."

"Y'all discussed adoption, and it wasn't what she wanted either?"

"Sure. I mean…she would have liked for us to look into it, but I wasn't about to get into a genetic crapshoot. She saw a counselor a few times and was fine."

"Did you ever go to a counseling appointment with her?"

"No." Nick seems puzzled. "She invited me, but she always scheduled them when I couldn't go. I tell you what, though, the Prozac really seemed to do the trick."

Here's where I have to be careful. Even though every person and couple is unique, there are certain patterns that show up time and time again. If I'm not careful, I can start making assumptions about this couple based on my past experiences. For instance, is Sam another dutiful wife who has made sacrifice after sacrifice for her husband with the hopes that someday he would just wake up and appreciate her? Is Nick another husband who assumes that if nothing's on fire, then everything must be great?

"Nick, this is a rather critical moment. I can probably be of some help, but I need to see if Sam will talk to me. In the meantime, it is very important that you find a way to sit in this pain. When we are this overwhelmed by anxiety, we often take reactive steps that just make things worse."

"I was going to tell her that if she didn't come home today that I was going to see my lawyer."

"That's exactly what I'm talking about. I'm thinking Sam has been sitting on a trash heap of pain for a long time, and has finally 'spoken.' If you want your marriage to have a chance, then you may need to sit for a while now."

"That doesn't sound very comforting." Is he irritated?

"Right now I'm choosing to believe that you want your marriage more than you want comfort."

"Fair enough." Is that a hint of recognition?

"Nick, sometimes 'I'm done' means exactly that. Sam may really be done with you. However, sometimes 'I'm done' means 'I love you, but I've flat run out of ideas for getting your attention.' I won't know where Sam is until, and unless, she will talk to me. What I often do in these situations is send an e-mail that says something like this:

Your husband has come to see me. I can be of much more help to him if I know more about how things look from your perspective. Would you be willing to come in, either alone or with Nick? Sometimes the spouse in your shoes wonders if she's somehow being manipulated into marriage counseling. If you are inclined to think this, then please let me assure you that this is not my intention.

"We've got to get her in here, doc." There's that desperation again…

"Actually, we don't. I suspect that, more than anything, Sam needs to know that her choices will be respected. If you push her, you may well lose her."

"Damn. Have I really been that big of an idiot?"

"Be careful what you ask me, Nick. I'm committed to being as honest as I can be with my clients." Nick first looks at me with sparks, but then seems comforted by my slight smile.

REFLECTIONS

Maybe we can understand Job's sudden cursing of his birth through Sam's eyes. We don't know enough, but it sounds like she had been building up resentment at the presumptuousness of her husband. One day, after the news of her inability to have children, she just exploded in the only way she knew how.

Maybe a character like Job, who had spent his life absorbing the injustices others might have committed, is an unstable emotional time bomb just waiting to explode. And finally, after the period of mourning his friends share with him, he feels permission from them to blow up. But he blows up in a way that holds God accountable and offends his friends.

We have all been in Nick's shoes, probably, asking ourselves how we could have been so blind to our own insensitivity toward someone we loved. Oddly enough, in the case of Job, we would like for God to voice those words: *How could I have been so insensitive to push Job to such extremes?* But, of course, this never happens in the story.

9

TELLING THE TRUTH IN COMMUNITY

JOB 4:17

Can mortals be righteous before God? Can human beings be pure before their Maker?

CONNECTIONS

Have you ever been in a Bible study class, or a worship service, and thought, *If these people knew what I really believed, they'd kick me out of this place!* Or perhaps more jarring, *If these people knew what went on in my home, they'd be shocked!* Honesty about faith is not just about what we believe, but also about how we live out, or fail to live out, these beliefs. Yet sometimes it seems that religious community is the *least* safe place for such honesty.

Job must share with his friends and they must respond with honesty, if not with integrity. The pastor of Tina and Mason must uphold the values of his community of faith on the matter of spousal abuse as revealed in the conversation below. We will hopefully think about whether their community of faith provides a safe place for such honesty.

THE HOMILY

Job is a book for both liberals and conservatives, because it portrays the search for truth in ways that are appealing to both. Now, liberals (let's call them progressives; some don't like to be called liberals) believe that truth is not objectively available. And so it is surfaced through debate and competing opinion. Conservatives, on the other hand, believe that truth is indeed objectively available, and that's because God (or Nature) makes it available to those who will but listen or look. The book of Job has them both, because it presents us with a great debate and relies upon God's appearance to settle the dispute. Job and his friends debate as though their lives depend upon it; and then God appears. The liberal interpreters of the book believe their claim is correct; what God actually says is open for interpretation, not known. The conservatives believe their claim is correct, because God's appearance alone is sufficient to settle Job's questions.

What makes this dialogue compelling to me is the picture Job and his friends present of *how* they tell the truth. When we begin to share honestly with others, all of the different assumptions we carry are evident. As much as we may claim that our faith is shaped by a religious tradition of some sort, we also carry many profoundly important individualistic assumptions.

God alone can search our individual hearts, we often say. On the other hand, part of what defines religious conviction is its being shared within a community of faith practice. This communal aspect means one cannot simply hold to beliefs alone. An individual must also share the opinions and practices of others in the community. In other words, and this is really tough for us North Americans, we actually have to listen to our friends who hold to the same religious values. We cannot simply decide on our own what God's revelation might or might not mean.

So, if the dialogue between Job and his friends has something for both conservatives and liberals, what is it? Well, there are several things. As far as community-building is concerned, we probably ought not to forget that the friends come and sit with Job in absolute silence for seven days, seeing that his suffering was so great (2:13). One well-known preacher has noted that even then they opened their mouths too soon.[5] But even more so, it is an act of community to join their friend in the search for truth. Their timing may have been inappropriate, but they are arguing with Job about something more important than all of them put together. There is obviously trust here, in that both Job and his friends are willing to take extraordinary risks to their friendships. Also, I think that Job's friends are committed to his good and not just their own. I am not denying that they have their own personal, individualistic motives, too. But, to engage in such a complex argument is more than merely about one's own personal motives. It is about Job's motives, too.

When Eliphaz drops this initial claim that it is impossible for humans to be justified before God, he is not arguing from Job's experience, but from a religious precept he takes to be authoritative. In fact, the authority stems from his own chilling revelatory experience (4:12-15). But Job, who is arguing from his experience, lays the basis for a serious disagreement. Job does not doubt that Eliphaz had such a revelation. Rather, he doubts it means what Eliphaz says it means. Such disagreement creates a significant potential rift in the community that might previously have existed between these friends.

It's not as though one can choose one over the other. One cannot say, I choose fellowship and will leave the religious precept alone, or *vice versa*. No, the complexity of communities of faith is that such precepts matter, because they partly form the basis for communities of faith. Job doesn't actually disagree with Eliphaz's claim (see 9:2, for instance). But unlike Eliphaz, Job sees it as a basis for *distrust* and *suspicion* of God. Now, can you have a fellowship based upon truth and also take such precepts in such different ways?

---

[5] Paul Duke, "First Prayer from the Ashes: A Sermon on Job 7:7-21," *Review & Expositor* 99 (Fall 2002): 615–19, attributes this to Gardner Taylor.

TINA AND MASON

If you kick an anthill, don't whine about getting bit.

RICHARD GAYLE

"Who the hell do you think you are?"

I've answered the phone, and it's a bit jarring for a conversation to start in this way.

"I'm sorry, but who is this?"

"This is Mason, Tina's husband."

"Oh, hello Mason. What's the problem?"

"I'll tell you what the hell the problem is. You sent the pastor to my house last night!"

Whoa. I guess this tells me which option Tina chose. I really didn't expect her to head in that direction.

"Well, Mason, I can assure you that I did not send the pastor to your house. I'm confused. Just what happened?"

"What happened is that the pastor and one of the elders showed up on my doorstep last night and got into my business."

I met Tina last week. She seemed like a zombie as she laid out the escalating abuse she was experiencing at the hands of her husband. Tina rolled up her sleeve to reveal an angry bruise on her upper right arm.

After I saw the bruise, I asked her, "So, Tina, when did things go from shoving to hitting?"

"Two nights ago," she answered in a monotone voice. "This was the first time he hit me. Things started getting bad about three months ago, right after he lost his job." I'm expecting at least a hint of emotion…

"And what was his temper like before that?"

"He's always been sort of explosive," she admitted. "We dated for two years before we got married, and he was so loving and respectful. I mean, I saw the way his dad treated his mom, which was scary. But Mason didn't seem anything like his dad. Once we got married, though, it's just been three years of me watching him build from a slow burn to this."

As Tina offered me more details about the past three years, I learned that she and Mason were members of the same "Bible Church" his family had helped start. His parents had moved away from the area, but Mason was respected as a young elder in the church. I'd met their pastor, and I considered him a thoughtful, strong leader. He and I would probably have trouble finding a lot in common theologically, but he clearly cared about his congregants, and didn't seem to have as much ego mixed up in his work as some pastors I've known. As Tina talked about her church, my curiosity began to rise.

"Tina, what do the folks at your church know about this?"

"I'd never talk to anyone at church about this. Mason would be horrified." Her eyes widen at the thought. "Plus, I doubt anyone would believe me. Folks there love Mason's momma and daddy. Mason's the youngest elder on the board, and he's head of the finance committee."

"You don't think your pastor could be of any help?"

"He's a good guy. He came a little over a year ago, right after Mason's parents moved, and he's spent a lot of time with Mason since he lost his job. I'd never tell him what's going on."

"Tina, we've touched on some of your options, and you've already told me that Mason has reacted almost violently when you asked him to go to couples counseling with you. I want to understand better why you discard the possibility of talking to your pastor. I've met him, and he seems solid to me. What I think I know about your church is that y'all take life together very seriously. I got the impression from your pastor that the notion of holding each other accountable is very important."

"I guess we talk that way." Tina seems to be coming out of her fog.

"But you don't trust it?"

"I just don't know. People don't put their personal lives on display for the preacher, do they?" I'm surprised by the hint of a smile that forms on her lips.

"Look, you are exactly right when you say that many, if not most, people put on a front at church. I'm just saying that it isn't wrong or bad for you to ask your pastor for help with something like this. I'm not telling you that it's what you *ought* to do. And it is certainly the sort of step that could send things off in all sorts of unexpected directions. I'm just saying that it's one of the options."

Tina is one of many people with whom I've had this type of conversation. It is incredibly rare for a person to choose to talk to the pastor. Back to the phone conversation…

"Mason, are you willing to listen as I explain a few things?

"Whatever."

"I can't talk to you about any conversation I might have had with your wife. But more importantly, I never tell anyone what to do. My job is to help my clients sort through their options. Sometimes they tell me what they are going to do before they leave my office. Sometimes they decide after they've left. If your pastor showed up at your house to talk to you about personal matters, it sure wasn't because I asked him to."

There's silence on the line, but I hear breathing. I continue.

"Just one other thing. Whenever an individual comes to me with a marriage problem, I'm always acutely aware that I'm hearing just one side of the story, and that things are almost always more complex than they first appear. I always ask my clients to invite the spouse to come with them. They almost always tell me that they've done so, but the spouse refused."

"I'm...well...I'm really pissed."

"Of course you are! It sounds like you were caught completely off guard, and that the conversation with your pastor and the elder was very uncomfortable for you. I figure I'm the last person you'd ever want any help from, but I'm available."

"Yeah...maybe...I don't know...The pastor and the elder said they expected me to make an appointment with a counselor soon...I need to think about this..."

"Mason, I've got to go, but I'm really glad you called. Most people just sit and burn in situations like this. Maybe we'll have a chance to meet in person sometime."

"I don't know...maybe...bye."

REFLECTIONS

Despite the contentiousness of conversations between Job and his friends, Milton is drawn to what their dialogue says about community particularly a *faith* community. He sees Job and his friends fighting to remain in community despite their disagreements over a core theological question: What is God like?

When I (Wes) first read Milt's homily, my mind went immediately to the tremendous anxiety that accountability arouses in churches, and how most congregations talk a better game than they live together.

A few years ago, I presented a case study to a group of pastors that was based on a true story. I asked the pastors to imagine that another respected minister in the community had called them, and that the conversation went like this:

> *Rev. Smith, a member of my congregation, is convinced that a member of your congregation has engaged in some very unethical business practices with him that has resulted in a large financial loss. If what my guy is telling me is basically accurate, it really doesn't reflect well on your guy. Anyway, he is intending to file a lawsuit, but said he'd be willing to have a meeting with the four of us to discuss this before he took that step.*

I guess I shouldn't have been shocked when most of the pastors said this was none of their business and would decline such a meeting.

10

GOD THE CONTENDER

JOB 10:2

I will say to God, Do not condemn me; let me know why you contend against me.

CONNECTIONS

Are you aware of your assumptions, the things you take for granted, about what is real? Our lives are ordered, in big and small ways, by our assumptions. If we could make no assumptions, then life would be impossibly stressful. You assume that when a stoplight is green for you, it is red for those coming from your left and right. Just imagine what driving would be like if you couldn't assume this!

The assumptions we make about traffic flow simplify life. The assumptions we make about relationships are much more complicated.

The implications of our images of God are life-changing. Job assumes that his image of God as judge is accurate, and he assumes that his definition of a fair judge should be the same as God's. The breakdown of this image is driving him mad. In the counseling session, Carter is feeling "crazy" based on his assumptions as well.

THE HOMILY

Theological language too often circulates without much thought among Christians. The language of God as judge betrays a common image of the deity of the monotheistic religions (Judaism, Christianity, and Islam). No matter how much loyalty, love, and mercy may be accompanying characteristics, God passes judgment upon his creatures. The word *contend* envisions a court hearing: Job believes God has initiated proceedings against him, treating him as though he had already been condemned. The problem to Job is that there has not even been a hearing. Evidence has not been laid out, neither have witnesses been called. No decision has been rendered. God has simply acted as the sole judge and executioner, without making things known to the one who is bearing the brunt of God's injustice.

Job is steeped in such a tradition. In his response to his second friend, Bildad, he breaks into the language of prayer and challenges God to *let me know why you contend against me* (10:2).

Of course, Bildad presses the metaphor further. He asks Job rhetorically whether it's even possible for God to pervert justice (8:3). And there we see the full-blown assumption that God is not only just, but that he presides over a universe that is just. Bildad goes on to point out to Job that the morally pure and virtuous are blessed and the morally impure are cursed. Bildad insists Job's circumstances can make perfect sense when viewed through this lens. Job's agony is a function of some kind of moral lapse Job has allowed, perhaps even unknowingly, and God is rendering judgment in the form of suffering. But you might ask what such a view really looks like; what does it mean to have a just God who acts as judge upon all of his creatures' moral actions? Answering such a question moves in the direction of fatuous analysis and extension of metaphorical language. Still, it might be interesting to think about the extended implications of some of our most cherished metaphorical religious language. Surely it would mean life lived out as though one were being watched all the time by heavenly beings in authority. One of my teachers playfully referred to such a deity as a divine peeping Tom. By further extension, having a just God could mean constantly living in fear of doing something wrong. One would have to be on guard at all times. The vigilance would also mean having to scrutinize one's thoughts endlessly, because the divine watcher would know one's thoughts or "search one's heart," to use the common religious language. And what about those moral choices one might make that are ambiguous, that have no clear right or wrong? Well, then life would be lived out either in fear of being wrong in such situations, or desperately searching for some word or sign that the heavenly judge was going to be lenient. Thus, I suppose, comes the need for God's mercy. But for some, such mercy comes at an almost impossibly high price: the price of never being free from God and thus alone with one's own thoughts and identity. At least Job himself wonders why God does not look away from him for just a while: *let me alone until I swallow my spit* (7:19).

I don't think that Job is calling for a new metaphor for God. Instead, I think he is trying to make the old metaphor, God as just contender, more workable. But I hear in his words the anguish analogous to those who say, I can't shut my thoughts off at night. It's possible that they are saying, "I cannot escape thinking of God as my judge." They may have been taught that when such anxiety occurs, God is a loving judge, a creator judge, but they know also that he is a judge nonetheless. And when I think of Jesus' life and work, I also wonder whether he was trying to offer some new metaphor, some new image by which people of faith could envision God. Perhaps Jesus was proposing that, Rather than think of God as contender, think of him as the one who gives up his own welfare for the welfare of others. But, of course, that's only a metaphor, too.

CARTER

Assumptions are the termites of relationships.

HENRY WINKLER

"Gawd, she pisses me off! She gets some Principal-of-the-Year award a couple of times and she starts acting like she owns the damn school!"

"I guess I don't need to ask, 'What's the right place for us to start today?'"

Carter first came to see me a couple of weeks before Christmas last year. He was the head of athletics at Crockett middle school in our community—a middle school with a particularly rough reputation. After the school had failed to meet minimum standards three years in a row, the superintendent had installed her star principal, Dr. Susan S., to lead Crockett. I have friends who know Dr. S. well, and they all describe her as a no-nonsense leader who knows how to get things done. She is also considered the consummate team player who doesn't expect anything of her teachers that she doesn't expect of herself. Carter had already let me know how shocked he was when Dr. S. had stepped in to substitute teach a couple of times when teachers had last-minute emergencies.

"Let's just say I had a rather intense meeting with the good doctor when school let out today. And to think I was excited when I first heard she was going to be our new principal."

"A meeting similar to the one you had with her right before you came to see me the first time?"

"Yeah. I just *thought* she was a bitch the first time." I'm aware of how his hands are shaped into fists.

According to Carter, he'd gotten a bit sloppy with his administrative duties during his time at Crockett, and he figured that the first meeting with Dr. S. was going to be about that. In fact, though, she was concerned about his lack of follow-through on calls to parents, and she had been rather pointed in expressing her priorities to him.

"Was this a follow-up meeting? We're…what?…about half-way through the spring semester?"

"This was the follow-up, and she is not a happy camper. I don't know what she expects, but it is evidently not what I'm doing. My paperwork is all up to speed for the first time since I can remember. I've attended every meeting I'm supposed to attend."

"So what was her gripe?"

"Phone calls…meetings with parents." Carter grips his head as though he feels a headache coming on. "What a colossal waste of time!"

"I don't understand."

"She's all into this 'personal touch' thing. At our first meeting, when she came on board, she asked all the teachers to identify twenty of the brightest 'at risk' students. Seven of them are involved in sports, so she told me she wanted me to take the lead with those students by getting to know their parents better…making calls to personally invite them to games, and to make sure I met them if and when they showed up."

"I remember you telling me about the focus on personal touch, but I don't recall you telling me the details of what you were expected to do. Did I miss something? We've been working on you getting your administrative act together."

"I know, and you've really helped me stay on point with that, but it's not enough for the doc."

"OK, but I'm confused. It sounds like you are telling me her top priority was getting teachers more personally connected with the parents of students. Again, did I miss something?"

Carter is silent. He looks like he just bit into a rotten peanut. I continue.

"Here's the picture that's beginning to take shape for me. A new sheriff rides into Dodge, and she lays out her plan and priorities for cleaning up the town. You've been focused on some of her goals, but have not been tending to her highest priority. She had one meeting with you to clarify her expectations. That meeting stressed you out enough to come see me, but you've never really made her highest priority one of your goals in our work. Is this about right?"

"Don't I pay you to be on my side?" Arms crossed now, Carter is serious.

"Now you've really got me confused. Are you paying me to help you keep your job, or paying me to help you feel better about losing your job?

Carter jerks his eyes to meet mine, and he can see that I'm smiling. A faint grin begins to form on his face.

"Well, when you put it like that…"

"You know, Carter, one of the issues I often run into with folks is their ambivalence about strong leadership. We all find some comfort in believing that a competent leader is in charge, but then we struggle to know what to do with ourselves when we find ourselves crossways with that leader. Some folks find it easier to question the competency of the leader than to look more closely at themselves. Is there even a chance that something like this is going on with you?"

"My wife tells me to either quit griping and do what the lady asks, or quit my job."

"Wait a second, you only get to surprise me once per session. You hadn't mentioned that your wife was irritated with you also. You'd given me the impression she was solidly in your corner."

"Well, she was, until more recently."

"We've just got a few minutes left, and I'd like to ask you to be thinking about a couple of things before we meet again. First, would you like for us to use some of our time focused on addressing the goals most important to your boss? Second, do you think it would be worth your time for us to explore a bit more how you drifted into such an adversarial perspective of your boss?

REFLECTIONS

I (Wes) regularly pass through a moderately traveled intersection in Waco where the stop signs were changed a couple of years ago. Previously the intersection was a four-way stop. The stop signs were removed on the east-west street. It is still comical to observe that intersection. I am often at the stop sign, waiting for the traffic to clear so I can cross, only to be amused (and irritated) by the number of drivers who still stop where there is no stop sign. What a simple, and powerful, testimony to the power of our assumptions.

Milton's homily highlights the power of unexamined, or subconscious, images. As Milt has already pointed out, the book of Job begins with a peek behind the curtain, revealing a picture of God that is troubling, to say the least. We then see how frustrating and misdirected the conversations can become when persons engage in theological debates over the nature of God and humans when none of them are in on what's happening behind the curtain. They all assume that it is indeed God's job to maintain order in the universe based on a fair set of rules. They don't have a way to think about a God who doesn't honor their preconceptions.

My conversation with Carter reflects countless sessions I've had with folks who are angry and scared because of a relationship with a strong leader. Certainly, some of these clients have been contending with capricious and unethical bosses who are asking them to step outside of their values in order to keep their jobs. But, perhaps more often than not, these clients don't know how to address their own insecurities in the face of both high expectations and the reality that their bosses have more things to consider than their happiness. Although I don't use the language of small self and Authentic Self in this conversation with Carter, the concepts are stamped all over it. The small self is always looking for a way to claim victim status.

11

WHEN JOB CHANGES HIS MIND

After these things, Job opened his mouth and cursed his day....

CONNECTIONS

Why do we change when we do? Why does one person stop smoking immediately after a heart attack, while another one continues to struggle with the habit that is killing him? How is it that a sense of peace can be obliterated in a moment for one person, and momentarily discovered by another?

The shift in the character of Job between chapters two and three is rather startling. It leaves many of us wondering what has happened to change Job's mind. In the counseling session, Parker's experience with a sunrise is very subtle. Both Job and Parker's reactions have something to do with the inner dialogue that accompanies their experiences. But when you read about someone else changing his mind, do you reflect upon what may be happening on the inside and not just on that which you see on the outside?

THE HOMILY

Why Job begins to curse is a judgment left up to each reader of the book. But there really would be nothing to talk about in the book of Job if the main character hadn't finally said something. We know that he had taken it from God and even justified doing so to his wife: *shall we receive good from God and not also receive evil?* (Job 1:10). We have seen how he is the quintessential faithful man, believing that...*the LORD loves justice; he will not forsake his faithful ones* (Psalm 37:28). We imagine him as knowing the traditions that have said, *The blessing of the LORD makes one rich, and he doesn't add pain with it* (Proverbs 10:22). So when Job opens up his mouth and curses his day, the day of his birth, we have to wonder what has brought this on. We get one clue in Job 3:23 when he describes his situation as God's having *hedged him in*. In this context, his words probably mean something like *blocked his way*. But Job's description forms a wonderful irony with the words of the satan who accuses God of *hedging Job in* in a good sense (1:10). The satan means to say that God's protective hedge is the very thing that Job is working to sustain. But reading these two verses against each other, we cannot help but wonder if there is not something that Job now sees about his former situation that makes him reject it. The unintended consequence of God's protection and blessing is beginning to believe the aim of faith is the blessing of God rather than Godself. We are not privy to the thoughts of the primal man and woman after they leave the garden as we are to Job's. But in some respects, like Job, they leave a life of blessing and take on an accursed life (see Genesis 3:14-24). The ground is cursed, so their toil is difficult. The woman is cursed, so childbirth is painful. The beast is cursed, so he lives in conflict with humanity. And the first episode of the couple's life outside the garden is the story of Cain and Abel (Genesis 4:1-16). Can you think of anything more accursed than having a son who kills his brother and is banished from his family and his country? I do wonder what Adam and Eve might have said as they looked back on the garden. Would they have intoned the words of Job: *Let the day of my birth perish...?* Or, would they have said, rather, that knowledge is always costly?

Remember, they traded paradise for wisdom and knowledge. And I would rather think how they might have been weighing the high cost over against the gains. In the garden, there was no real independence; they apparently were prevented from attaining wisdom; and, they still had to die (the tree of life was off limits, too [Genesis 3:22]). Perhaps they might have been saying, *Thank God, we've been set free from all of that!* Yes, we have to take responsibility for our lives. But we make our own choices now, and life, though cursed, is full of new possibilities we could never have dreamed before. Isn't that the language of an adult? And when adults are finally ready to venture out of the garden, they are embracing a life that constantly counterpoises the eternal pulls of childhood versus adult responsibility.

Is it possible that when we see Job's sudden change of mind, he is not only cursing the pain of his current situation but also the limitation, the ignorance, the closed-mindedness of his former situation? And from that point of view, his arguments are attempts to understand the new against the old.

PARKER

Maybe it's all utterly meaningless. Maybe it's all unutterably meaningful. If you want to know which, pay attention to what it means to be truly human in a world that half the time we're in love with and half the time scares the hell out of us.

FREDERICK BUECHNER

"Yeah, I guess it was good, but it's always nice to get back home."

I had to smile. Who else, but Parker, would describe a month of traveling around the country with such ambivalence.

"Did you and your buddy have any fist fights? Traveling and camping can stress a friendship."

"We did fine. Jimmy and I have been best friends since junior high. We're a pretty good team. Though I must admit I got sick of his devotion to conservative talk radio."

I do find it a little hard to imagine Parker camping. He's the caricature of his job as a philosophy professor, always dressed professionally, yet managing to look a bit disheveled. When he told me that he and his best friend from childhood were going on this trip, his seeming lack of enthusiasm for the adventure was notable. But I'd already concluded that Parker had been depressed for a long, long time.

"Did you get to all the places on your itinerary?"

"Yes, we did. Except for a few changes in the roads, we repeated the same trip we took together the summer after graduating from high school. We both kept saying, 'Can you believe it's been thirty years?'" Parker is shaking his head as though he's still with Jimmy.

"It sounds like such great fun."

"I guess so, but I was never quite able to shake that deep sense of unrest that brought me in here last fall." He suddenly seems so sad...

"I'm sorry to hear that. I know you were hoping this trip would reawaken some of your zest for life."

"I keep thinking about that kid outside of Little Rock. We'd discovered a tire was losing air at a rest stop a few miles back, so we took the next exit and headed toward town. When we pulled into the first station there was this kid, seventeen or eighteen years old, sitting on a stool. Jimmy can be such an ass."

"What?"

"The kid glances at the tire and says, 'Gettin' a flat? Jimmy says, 'Actually, we keep letting the air out, but it won't stop filling itself back up.' The kid didn't get it."

"That's funny. Sort of cruel, but funny."

"I guess so. Anyway, after we found a place to plug the tire, we were back on the road. Jimmy reflected, 'Aren't you glad we didn't end up like that kid?' All I could think was what a relief it would be to never have had an original thought."

We sit in silence as those words hang in the air. Then Parker continues.

"I know this is something a philosophy professor would say, but that kid brought into focus everything we've been talking about."

"How so?"

"Why did I have to be the 'brilliant' one? Who decided that intelligence was such a gift?" He is almost spitting these words. "Why did my parents decide it was such a huge deal that I'd gotten a couple of poems and essays published in *Atlantic Magazine* before I graduated? Who cares if I've published six books when I end up envying some high-school dropout?"

"And yet everyone expects you to feel like the most blessed man on the planet?"

"Yeah…yeah…like the most blessed freak on the planet. Yet, I've got to admit, I had your voice in my head on this trip." His eyes laser in on me, like… an accusation?

"That sounds disturbing. What do you mean?" I laugh, a bit uneasily.

"You know how annoyed I get with you when you say, 'Pay attention to what you notice.'"

"I have indeed said that to you a few times. I've never had the impression you noticed that suggestion."

"Well, I heard you in my head several times on this trip. One morning we'd gotten on the road while it was still dark. I was driving. Jimmy was sleeping. I was all wrapped up in my angst when I heard your words: *Pay attention to what you are noticing.* Suddenly I'm aware that the sun is halfway up, and the sky is filled with amazing colors. I swear, I felt this sort of mystical peace for a few moments."

"For a few moments?"

"Well, yeah." He laughs. Because next I thought, 'Damn, why'd you have to miss the first half of that sunrise?'"

"Dang, Parker, Adam and Eve only got kicked out of the garden once. You seem to boot yourself out on a regular basis!"

"I know…I know." Still laughing, Parker seems to have touched his absurdity.

"And I know you almost always feel sort of victimized by what your mind does to you—as though you have no choice in the matter. You actually didn't have much choice as a child. Your parents evidently needed for you to be amazing, and so they pushed you along. Yet, as much as you've resented your parents for that, haven't you just taken over the job of pushing yourself?"

"I suppose I have. Yes… yes… that's exactly what I've done." I'm surprised by how relaxed Parker seems to be as he owns himself.

"May I ask another, potentially annoying, question?"

"I suppose you may."

"Are you ready to be a better parent to yourself?"

REFLECTIONS

I (Wes) approach Parker with the assumption that he believes his inner evaluations of his experiences and of himself actually say something about reality. Therapy is often a slow dance with these assumptions—a process of raising these assumptions into awareness so the individual can make fresh decisions about how much power he will allow them to have. Are you really required to miss the beauty of a sunrise because you resent the expectations your parents placed on you as a child?

Therapy provides a setting in which to examine our assumptions, but Job wasn't seeing a therapist. We can only speculate about the inner dialogue that led him from seeming acceptance to an eruption of anger. I (Milton) can imagine several different sorts of conversations he could have had with himself. What might it have been like if he'd had someone around who didn't have an ax to grind, but was gently asking him to notice what he notices?

There is also the tendency for us to put the poet of Job on the therapist's couch. We want to know what the writer has been noticing in the world. In fact, we would really like to know what provoked the poet to write this set of dialogues riffing on the old story of Job. What anger does the main character, Job, allow the writer to voice?

Milton: I really like what you say about therapy: "a slow dance with these assumptions." I resist, though, trying to suggest that reading the story of Job is a form of putting the poet of Job on the therapist's couch. We just don't have enough detail in the story. Further, why would we risk reading such approaches back into the story of Job?

Wes: Aren't you just resisting your own imagination, though? You've admitted above that you could "imagine" several conversations Job the character could be having with himself. By doing that, aren't you putting the character and perhaps the poet on your own kind of therapeutic couch? The scholar's couch? You just don't like my kind of therapy.

Milton: Well, I've never thought of it that way. But even if I were doing that, I at least know where boundaries have to be drawn around what such imagination signifies. I mean, the biblical text is finite. It cannot mean anything. People who think it does use it to defend everything from deficit spending to the second amendment.

Wes: I don't doubt you on that, but I just feel that by limiting what the text can mean, you are actually trying to control meaning and control imagination. In a sense you are like Parker, reluctant to notice what you notice. The text evokes extraordinary emotional responses as we imagine these conversations between Job and God, Job and his friends, and Job and himself. We should go with those things. In fact, haven't I heard you say that the ancient notion of inspiration was that the text came from God and therefore its meaning was not constrained by the mere words of the text? That's why it *could* speak to successive generations of readers.

12.

SUFFERING IN OUR HEADS

JOB 3:25

Truly the thing I fear comes upon me, and what I dread befalls me.

CONNECTIONS

What does *acceptance* mean to you? One can't read from the mystics of any of the world's prominent religious traditions without running into the word over and over. Acceptance is not something Job is able to do; that at least seems certain. His seemingly endless descriptions of both emotional and physical pain would suggest that he has had much different expectations for his life than what his current situation provides. Perhaps his expectations are part of his problem. But then, hasn't his religious tradition taught him to have such expectations?

Language is so powerful. It joins forces with our culture to shape us; in that way it feeds and shapes our expectations. The word *Parkinson's* can have a powerful emotional effect. It certainly does on Jane in the following scenario. But language is what makes up much of our world, and nothing illustrates how made-up our social worlds are like reflecting upon the meaning of "getting the knack of hopelessness."

THE HOMILY

Does emotional wellness shape the way we see things? Our attention is easily drawn to the physical suffering of Job without considering the emotional suffering. It's a common oversight reinforced by western civilization's biases. It's fairly easy to go through the litany of Job's many losses: his oxen and donkeys, his sheep and servants, his camels, his kids, and finally his health. All of these things have real political significances, too. His livestock was understood in ancient economies as his wealth. His servants were not only wealth, but a significant contribution to the economy, also. Job's children had more than sentimental value; they were his future, as his livelihood was theirs. Likewise, the social status of his wife stemmed from her husband as well as her children, especially her male children. So, we know without having to intuit much that Job's losses are powerfully important. And loss of his physical health is both provocative as well as foreboding. Identification of his disease seems impossible. It is probably best to rely on a broad designation of Job's illness as some kind of chronic skin disease that has open, painful sores that repeatedly erupt (7:5), turn black, and peel off (30:30). But we cannot avoid the descriptions of the physical pain that Job is in as a result: he is wasting away physically (19:20), has a continuous fever (30:30b), has trouble sleeping (7:14), and cries all of the time (16:16). He is presented to us as feeling this pain in his bones (30:17), thus it is deep, deep pain across his entire body.

I am fearful that many readers seek to downplay the emotional distress that Job feels along with all of this physical pain, though. Of course, it is we moderns who like to separate the physical from the emotional, despite the fact that our brain is the central monitor and interpreter for both. In some sense the ancient treatment of suffering without separating out the physical from the emotional is more accurate physiologically. Nevertheless, Job talks about a lot of suffering that is neither physical nor forensic. He may be suffering injustice, but we too often blithely gloss over the other kinds of suffering he experiences. When Job talks about his fear and dread (3:25; 7:14), we immediately wonder whether the fear and dread accompany him in his current state of calamity, or if it was present prior to his disastrous fall. Why does it matter to us, though? It would be perfectly understandable for a man who is experiencing such physical pain on top of the loss of everything to be afraid of what might happen next. Terrifying dreams and frightening visions (7:14) would make sense. On the other hand, is it possible that the reference is to his days of health and prosperity, and the secret harboring of a deeply seated fear of what *could* happen if he lost everything? What would that say about his trust in God?

What does Job mean when he speaks of the anguish of his spirit, and the bitterness of his soul (7:11)? When he says his spirit is broken (17:1), isn't he referring to the emotional distress that he is in? He's vexed about his situation (6:2); isn't he talking about the way he feels? He's angry, perplexed, feels harassed, irritated, and uncertain about what to do. He doesn't know what to do, because he doesn't know whom to trust. He thinks his friends are false (6:16-18). He thinks God has caused all this and has behaved not only unjustly, but also like an overpowering bully (9:17-20). His spirit, he says, drinks the poison of God's arrows (6:4). There is no rejoicing, no exultation. His soul is bitter, he says (10:1). Job is thinking about much more than his physical suffering. The serious emotional aspects of his calamity cannot be relegated to a secondary position. Rather, his emotional distress should be at the center of our gaze.

JANE

Turning your mind towards [God[6]] does not bring security or confirmation. Turning your mind towards [God] does not bring

---

[6] I (Wes) have replaced Chödrön's words "the Dharma" with "God" in order to make the quote more understandable to those unfamiliar with Buddhist terminology. My apologies to those who believe this to be an inappropriate rendering of Dharma, but after some research I was comfortable with it.

any ground to stand on. In fact, when your mind turns toward [God], you fearlessly acknowledge impermanence and change and begin to get the knack of hopelessness.

PEMA CHÖDRÖN

Jane is so agitated she can hardly sit. An attractive and dignified woman in her early sixties, Jane finally came to see me to get her adult children off her back. Six months prior, she'd simply fallen down in the children's section of Old Navy while scouring the clearance rack. (She loved finding bargains for her grandchildren.) When she mentioned the tumble to her son, he'd insisted she see a doctor. He'd been noticing an odd limp in her gait and the occasional illogical remark that she'd make. His fears were confirmed when the diagnosis eventually was made: Parkinson's.

The disease had progressed quickly. Her son and daughter watched their very active mother retreat into the dark corners of her small home, and they were worried. She agreed to see me, not for herself, but to ease the anxiety of everyone else.

This was our fifth appointment, and she'd finally dropped her I-don't-understand-why-everyone-is-so-concerned act.

"Why won't God just let me die?" The words were slurred, yet jarring.

"No one has a clue the hell you live with every day, do they?"

Jane looks at me like I'm an imbecile.

"I never thought I'd survive the death of my child in 1967. I never thought I'd survive the bankruptcy in 1982. I never thought I'd survive Raymond's death five years ago. No one thinks about those charming events when they say stupid things like, 'Oh, your children and grandchildren must be such a blessing at a time like this.'"

I'm silent. I don't think I could move a muscle even if a fire broke out.

"And what's with that ridiculous 'encouragement card' I picked up on the way out the door last week? You call that encouragement?"

I'd wondered what Jane would make of that one when I saw her take a card out of the holder next to the waiting-room door. Last week's card was a quote from Pema Chödrön, a Buddhist monk. "What does that mean, 'getting the knack of hopelessness?' That doesn't sound like anything I've read in the Bible," she says.

"Have you ever read Psalm 88? Unlike so many of the Psalms that begin with despair and end with an affirmation of God's power and care, number 88 just starts in the ditch and ends in the ditch. One of the most uplifting lines is:

You have put me in the lowest pit.
In dark places, in the depth.
Your wrath has rested upon me,
And you have afflicted me with all your waves.

"Isn't that sweet." The words drip with sarcasm, regardless of her slurring speech.

"Jane, scripture is full of expressions of anger and hopelessness. And, it seems to me, the hopelessness is fueled by our expectation that life should be different from what it is. Or at least that *my* life should be different from what it is. I've always thought that's what Pema is getting at with 'getting the knack of hopelessness.' Authentic hope starts with an acceptance of hopelessness. Do you suppose this applies at all to you? There's no denying the suffocating pain you have been through and live with every day. Yet, do you suppose your pain is amplified by a belief that life should not be this way?"

"If you're telling me to 'get over it,' then I'm walking out of here and never coming back," she snaps.

"Oh Jane, I would never dishonor you with such triviality. I know what it's like to want to die, and I know what it's like to be peppered with idiocy from people who didn't know what to do with me. But I also know that all of the great spiritual teachers seem to agree that any chance for genuine peace begins with a radical acceptance of what *is*."

"So I'm supposed to just smile as I progressively lose my bodily and mental abilities?"

Jane's question doesn't have an edge to it. It seems to reflect genuine curiosity.

"Contentment is not about denial, Jane. It's not about pretending. Contentment has something to do with feeling the pain, and yet marveling at your granddaughter on the stage as she plays the lead role in her high school play."

We both notice the clock. Jane stands to go....

REFLECTIONS

Psalm 88 is an intriguing lens through which to read the lamenting of Job's words. It is true that it starts in a ditch and ends in a ditch. However, there is that opening cry in 88:1, where the sufferer refers to God as "God of my salvation." That may be the only word of hope in the whole psalm, and it probably could equally serve as an accusation.

We do wonder what kind of salvation one could have who also claims that he is "Wretched and close to death from my youth up..." (v. 15). Jane's chronic degenerative disease probably makes her feel wretched. But, of course, these are just words that people put on her condition; words are interpretative. Is she searching for some new language by which to be remembered?

In fact, it makes me (Milton) wonder what role simply finding new language might play in going through crisis. Language shapes us. We are, as N. Scott Momaday wrote, "men made of words."

13

DOES WORLDVIEW MATTER?

JOB 5:1

"Call now; is there anyone who will answer you? To which of the holy ones will you turn?"

CONNECTIONS

Again, we begin with a question about assumptions: *Has anything you've read in this book, so far, challenged yours?* We *hope* so, though we don't *assume* you'll feel compelled to change them.

This homily again examines the assumptions held by Job and by his friends. Job and Eliphaz may share common assumptions, but those will be challenged when God finally speaks. How much do both of them challenge those assumptions before God ever opens God's mouth?

In the counseling session, Max and Charlene are trapped in the assumptions about the moral order of the universe. We see how hard it can be for a person to take a fresh look at her beliefs, despite how much suffering her rigid beliefs are inflicting on her partner.

THE HOMILY

We seldom reflect upon the possible differences of worldview between the poet of Job and contemporary civilization. Eliphaz continues his initial council to Job by questioning whether there is anyone, presumably in the heavens, who will answer his cries: *Call now, is there anyone who will answer you? To which of the holy ones will you turn?* (5:1). And you may recall that Eliphaz has already insisted that God has "servants" and "messengers" (4:17; 5:5), though he puts no particular trust in them vis-à-vis humanity. Perhaps these are the "heavenly beings" or "sons of God" that are referred to in the opening scenes of the story (1:6; 2:1), and which Job could be invoking to curse the sea and rouse up Leviathan's chaos (3:8). Perhaps it's them to which Elihu refers in 33:32 as those who intervene on humanity's behalf in times of trouble. There's no way to know for certain.

Certainly the poet of these dialogues has constructed a story-world in which such beings exist and may come to the aid of humanity at God's bidding. But the presence of these beings in the story presents us with a fundamental problem of worldview. Do you live and practice your religious faith in a worldview that admits such beings exist? And do you have to believe in such beings in order for your religious faith to be effective?

I remember how I first encountered the idea of a worldview. In an undergraduate German class, we came across the word *Weltanschauung*. Of course, our instructor was not interested in the philosophical origins of the term, but said that it was a loan-word that came into English as "worldview." *Weltanschauung* means one's total outlook on the world—one's fundamental beliefs, assumptions, knowledge, and values that influence the way one behaves. And, as I have reflected a bit on it, it seems that the word has become more and more popular among religious folk as a means of differentiating themselves from other religious folk: "Well, she has a different worldview than we do"; or "Muslims have a different worldview from Christians." And for that matter, the Qu'ran is indeed explicit in its requirement that Muslims believe in angels (Sura 2:97-100). While the Bible also reinforces belief in angels, contemporary readers may not themselves have a worldview that includes such beings.

How foreign it must seem to encounter this reference in Job 5:1 if you do not have a worldview that admits such angels and heavenly intermediaries. In fact, the best we may be able to do here is simply acknowledge how different this very ancient cosmology is from our own modern cosmology. And in offering that acknowledgment, one still may stand in awe that somehow such ancient texts with such ancient cosmologies continue to speak and have some relevance.

I think, though, that encountering such a foreign worldview is perhaps healthy for readers of Job. God challenges Job on his own worldview. When God finally speaks, he implicitly accuses Job of speaking with words without knowledge (38:2). And, moreover, Job discovers that he has been wrong about his own worldview. The issue is not about the existence of angels, but it is about a view at the heart of the Hebrew literature. Justice as a principle of universal governance, God seems to suggest in his responses to Job, does not exist. And which is more important to us: that there are not angels or that there is not justice?

MAX AND CHARLENE

And since they did not see fit to acknowledge God, God gave them up to a debased mind and to things that should not be done. They were filled with every kind of wickedness…They know God's decree, that those who practice such things deserve to die…

ROMANS 1:28-32

"Well, he's addicted to porn and dragging our entire family out from under God's blessing. *That's* the problem."

Max droops like a chastised child as Charlene aggressively opens our conversation. I suspected this could be interesting when I learned the pastor of a charismatic congregation in town had referred this couple to me. I'd met the pastor a couple of years ago at some social gathering, and he'd made it clear he didn't hold my profession in the highest regard. I never expected that he would send someone my way. So I figured, perhaps unfairly, that he must really be frustrated with these two.

"What do you mean, Charlene?" I ask.

"The Bible says that God will just turn reprobates over to their lusts. If God has turned his back on Max, then our whole family is at risk."

"Max, what's your take on things?"

Max seems almost startled to have been invited into the conversation.

"Well, she's right." I can barely hear the words as he squeaks them out. "I've been looking at bad stuff on the computer. I told her I've stopped, and I feel just awful about it. She told the kids, though, and they're pretty upset. I've created a real mess."

"Charlene, you told your kids about this?"

"Yes, I did. They may all be out on their own now, but they have a right to know that our entire family has been spiritually compromised."

Yikes! I feel my anger rising, and yet I also know that I'm feeling a bit like a hypocrite. How often have I cautioned others against judging someone's view of God and interpretation of scripture? Yet, isn't Charlene clearly using her religion to inflict as much pain as she can on her husband? I'm going to have to sort through this some more with a colleague.

"Charlene, just so I can understand your concerns better, where does the notion of God's grace fit in to the equation for you?"

"Scripture says that some people are beyond God's grace."

"If that's the case, do you know why you're still with Max, trying to get him to change?"

For the first time, Charlene seems to be without words. But she recovers...

"Are you saying I should divorce him?"

"No, I don't think so. I'm just aware of what a horrible bind you are in. You would clearly be against divorce, and yet you seem convinced that Max is beyond redemption. You must feel completely trapped."

Again, Charlene is silent for a moment, so I turn to Max.

"Max, I suppose you could be as far gone as Charlene fears, but you wouldn't be the first good man who has struggled with something like this and been completely baffled by his urges and impulses. What are you thinking?"

"I'm thinking I'm an awful person…a horrible man." I didn't think he could sink any deeper into my worn couch.

I am very cautious about asking Max questions with Charlene present. I'm convinced that anything he says will potentially be used against him, yet I'm doubtful that he and I will get the opportunity to talk alone.

"Max, I suppose you could be one of the reprobates Paul is talking about in Romans, but I also have talked with a lot of men struggling like you are, and almost all of them tell stories of pain and confusion… things that have happened to them along the way that they've never talked about. Does that fit you?"

"You mean stories like when the neighborhood kid messed with me when I was about seven, or when I found my dad's stash of *Playboys* when I was twelve?"

Charlene interjects, "You've never told me any of this."

My anxiety continues to rise, not because Max has revealed himself, but because he has done so in front of a wife who is so graceless and aggressive. I remain focused on Max.

"Yeah, Max, that's the sort of stuff I'm talking about. We've all had painful experiences that can affect our spiritual growth, especially if we've never had a chance to sort through them. Do you suppose it would be helpful for you and me to discuss some of this?"

Max looks to Charlene, and I have the distinct impression he is seeking permission. Not only has she not softened, she looks even angrier, which I wasn't sure was possible until now. Charlene speaks next.

"This is ridiculous. He needs to face his sins, not make excuses for them."

"We would all do well to face our sins, Charlene. My recommendation is that Max and I spend some time, just him and me, sorting through this a bit more. Max, what would you like to do?"

Max is immobilized. He looks pleadingly at me, and then at Charlene. He can't seem to get any words out. Again, Charlene speaks.

"We'll have to talk about this and get back to you."

"Max, you know where to find me if you want to follow up on what I've suggested."

On rare occasions, the Maxes who cross my threshold do indeed call me again, but Max does not. He still crosses my mind from time to time.

REFLECTIONS

When I (Wes) was a much younger man, I met an evangelist who, upon observing all the drilling rigs in Oklahoma, commented, "I don't know what we're going to do if they drill deep enough to tap into hell and release the demons." I thought he was joking, but the serious expression that remained on his face suggested otherwise. I've since learned that it's virtually impossible to hold a meaningful conversation with someone who maintains a radically different worldview from my own. I've never encountered anyone in therapy who held such a view of the physical world as this evangelist, but I rather routinely encounter persons who are locked into a theological worldview that, from where I stand, seems very out of sync with the Jesus we encounter in the gospels.

I (Milton) am really appreciative of the counselor's being portrayed as self-aware and reflective of his own biases, especially when he acknowleges that he feels somewhat like a hypocrite: *How often have I cautioned others against judging someone's view of God and interpretation of scripture?* And yet, isn't that exactly what we are doing? We are making judgments based upon these exchanges, much like Job and his friends are doing. We cannot get away from it. Making judgments about other people's perspectives on the world is a strategy of our own health, no?

14

Admitting the Motive of Fear

JOB 6:21B

You see my calamity, and are afraid.

Connections

How well do you understand your motivation to help others? We'd all like to believe that we are motivated by love, by our genuine concern for the one we are helping. Yet, how can you be sure that you are not driven by darker, or at least less mature, motives?

Notice how Job probes beneath the surface of his friends' motives. He suspects their concern is not driven by their love for him, but rather by their fear that Job might actually be right. Consistent with the Job we've come to know, he pulls no punches. He accuses them of hiding behind their religion.

Skillful counselors invite, and sometimes provoke, their clients to examine their inner fears. Have you ever wondered, though, how the counselor's own fears might be in play? In Owen's case, we are asked to consider how his own backstage area silently motivates his attitudes toward one of his clients.

THE HOMILY

Why would Job think that his friends' words of comfort arise from their fear rather than their love? A colleague recently shared with me one of his teaching goals: *That students read at least one life-changing book in their four-year experience.* That's not much to ask, really, I thought. But then I tried to recall whether that had happened to me in my four years at school. I'm not sure.

There is one book I recall frequently enough, but whether it changed my life, who can know? I read Erving Goffman's *The Presentation of Self in Everyday Life* (1959) when it was already seventeen or eighteen years old. Goffman asserts that people's lives are lived out as though they are scripted by their social roles. Daily exchanges and interactions between friends, families, and fellow-workers are dramatic presentations. Each person is an actor of sorts, wearing a kind of mask that goes along with her or his role-playing. I remember Goffman's description of the *backstage*—that area we protect and allow very few to see. The backstage is where we are most vulnerable and have to be most honest.

Job accuses his friends of being afraid when they see him, but what could that possibly mean? The accusation comes as the conclusion to a series of metaphors Job applies to his friends. He insists that their friendships are like unreliable Palestinian *wadi* beds (6:15-20). During the season of rain, they are gushing and water is plentiful. But during the dry months, the once vast course of water is gone with not a drop anywhere. Job envisions caravans cutting across the desert areas in need of refreshment, and turning off the main road to find water, only to arrive and find the dry *wadi*. This metaphor explains Job's perception of their change in behavior, but it does not explain his accusation of fear.

Could it be that Job's friends have unexpectedly ventured into his backstage? It's almost unavoidable since all of the social role-playing that defined Job's existence has been undercut by his calamity. Nothing is left but his own *nakedness* (1:21). Nakedness occurs throughout biblical literature as a vivid image of vulnerability, exposure, and weakness. For instance, Joseph, as a powerful administrator in Egypt, accuses his brothers of being spies who were there only to discover the *nakedness of the land* (Genesis 42:9).

So Job believes his friends are more terrified than anything else. Like them, Job once had great wealth and power. If he could lose everything, couldn't they? Seeing it in a close friend no doubt confronts the friends with their own vulnerability, which they must protect in the backstage. They need to believe that Job is different from them. They need to believe that what has happened to Job could never happen to them.

If this interpretation has any merit, then Job's friends were trying to help him in order to save their own sanity and ease. Oh, I'm sure they were truly concerned about Job's suffering to an extent. But, if this scenario is correct, we are forced to reflect upon the backstage areas that each of us protects. What is more, we might ask whether our practice of religious faith is something that simply covers the *nakedness of a thing* or helps us embrace fully the backstage areas of our lives as they relate to the presentations we make in front of everyone else.

Owen

Be not angry that you cannot make others as you wish them to be, since you cannot make yourself as you wish to be.

THOMAS À KEMPIS

"Owen, let's get back to basics. Anger is always a response to a threat. I've not seen you this angry over a client before. What's the threat?"

In less than six months, Owen will have completed the requirements to become a licensed professional counselor. I've been supervising his work and enjoying the time with him tremendously. I first met Owen about ten years ago, when I was teaching a class at the seminary. He'd stood out as a curious and thoughtful student who asked great questions. When he contacted me a couple of years ago about supervising his work toward licensure, I was glad to take him on. He's pushed me as much as I've pushed him.

"The guy is setting himself up. His wife has hardly followed through on any of her promises. If he moves back home now, then it's all going to blow up in his face."

"You may be right. You are *probably* right. But when I listen to this recording, I hear your voice rising as it becomes clear what your client is going to do. When he says, *So you think I'm an idiot, right?* you go silent. Do you recall what was going through your mind in that silence?"

It is a common practice for supervisees to record sessions with a client, always with the client's permission. Owen typically asks me to listen to the most difficult moments in his work. He's not afraid to reveal his struggles with learning this craft, and I admire him for that. This supervision session is different, though. I think this is the first time Owen wanted me to affirm his stance more than he wanted to learn something.

"Well, what I suspect was going through my mind was, *How do I tell this guy I actually do think he's an idiot?*"

"That's what I'm curious about. It's not like you to come off as judgmental as you do in this conversation. What is it about this particular client in this particular situation that has your small self doing back flips?"

"The guy's been putting up with all sorts of horrible abuse from his wife for years. I've spent months helping him strengthen his resolve to a place where he could stand up for himself. I told him that she might not take him seriously until he moved out, and I nailed it. He read that blog post you wrote on leaving your spouse while you're still in love,[7] and things started making sense to him. He told her he was ready to leave if she didn't get some help. She ignored him. He moved out. She threatened divorce. He held his ground, and she began to shift. Damn.

---

[7] See http://practicalspirituality.wordpress.com/2008/07/20/
leave-your-spouse-while-you-are-still-in-love-part-1/

I think this is some of the best work I've done, and he's going to throw it away."

"He's going to throw away *your* work?"

Owen leans back in the chair. I see him searching his thoughts. When he speaks, his voice has regained its typical softness.

"He's going to throw away *my* work."

"What work of *yours* is he going to throw away?"

"Who knows for sure, but I can tell you where my mind just went. You know that my childhood was scarred by my dad's drinking, but I don't think I ever told you about the time mom finally kicked him out. I think I was fourteen, and dad had shoved me down during some stupid argument we were having. It was the first time he'd actually laid a hand on me, and mom flipped. She told him to get out or she was calling the police. He left."

"She stood up for you."

"She stood up for herself, but it only lasted about three weeks. Those were three wonderful weeks of peace in our home. And then he was back. Mom said he'd stopped drinking and was attending AA. All I could think was, *How could anyone change in three weeks?*"

"Had he changed?"

"Not really. He wasn't drinking, at least not in front of us, but I could still smell the beer on him from time to time. The house was full of tension again, but I guess it was OK enough for mom."

"Don't you hate it when that happens?"

"Yeah, I hate it when people don't expect more for themselves."

"That's not what I meant. Don't you hate it when our clients accidentally shine a spotlight on our own backstage issues?"

Again, Owen is quiet as he soaks this in.

"I see what you mean. But don't you agree that it's a mistake for my client to move back home this soon?"

"Probably, but I'm not sure that's the point right now. Next time let's talk about what it's like when our clients don't have a need to achieve as much *health* as we'd like them to. For now, I'd recommend that you sit a bit more with what you're discovering about how your wounds can become mixed up with the wounds of your clients."

REFLECTIONS

It's always risky to project our modern sensibilities onto biblical stories, but when Milton suggests a somewhat psychoanalytic angle for the relationship between Job and his friends, I (Wes) think he's on to something. Like it or not, we all bring a history to our relationships. We all construct a story to help us make sense of our histories and, sometimes, our stories are threatened by the way others construct theirs. This is one reason why living out an ethic of sacrificial love requires discipline, self-reflection, and community.

I (Milton) am caught up in Wes's concluding word, *community*. When we begin to consider how our backstage areas complicate the relationships we hold in community, we may be venturing into an area of greatest difficulty. Can you imagine being as honest with those in your faith community as occurs between a counselor and client, or a counselor and supervisor? While I doubt that the poet of Job envisions such a depth of self-disclosure, my own hidden assumptions drive me to reflect upon how a community of faith might explore together those areas of selfhood they prefer to protect at all cost.

15

Lying for God's Sake

Job 13:7-12

Will you speak falsely for God, and speak deceitfully for him? Will you show partiality toward him? Will you plead the case for God?

Connections

Have you ever spoken *falsely for* God? Be careful if you are inclined to answer *no.*

This homily reflects upon a passage where Job accuses his friends of defending God's cause to the extent that they cannot admit the reality of Job's own experience. It is a kind of lying that they are participating in for the sake of their traditional religious faith.

The counselor accuses Carson of essentially doing the same thing by confusing his desire for a divorce from his wife with his questioning about whether God really exists. The latter question is important, but having faith that there is a God and deciding whether divorce are two issues Carson needs to deal with separately.

THE HOMILY

Pleading God's case is one way to think about what professional ministers do. I hasten to say that this is not mudslinging from the back pew. I include myself as a participant in this hopefully noble profession. Sadly, though, not everyone would agree that *noble* is an accurate adjective. Even my eighth-grade English teacher cracked wise when I informed him and my class, in one of those excruciating moments of adolescent self-disclosure, that my father was a minister. I don't recall everything he had to say, but I believe this was the first time I'd heard the word *asinine*. I began to realize that not all people admire the way ministers speak on God's behalf.

Job accuses his friends of "speaking falsely for God, and speaking deceitfully for him..." (12:7). This isn't just someone complaining about the TV preacher who is begging for alms in the name of God's will. Job believes he has a legal case against God (13:3; 9:3), and he also believes his friends are breaking the rules of procedure by taking God's side. The Covenant Code, with which the original readers of this book might have been familiar, is unambiguous regarding the rules for those acting as witnesses in a courtroom. A witness must tell the truth. A witness must not simply side with majority opinion, or show favor based on the economic status of those involved (Exodus 23:1-3). Job is calling his friends out. He asserts that they are unfit to speak since they cannot be unbiased.

Can you imagine a person having to defend his statements about God in the same way a witness must defend statements in a courtroom? We ministers, who preach and teach on a regular basis, are almost never in positions where we have to be cross-examined about the testimonies we give. How would you handle such a cross-examination? Could you speak what you believe about God and faith without *lying*? Remember, in a courtroom setting, a lie is anything you might say that you can't back up with facts. How would you talk about your faith under such circumstances?

I think that both Job and his friends thought, as they burrowed deeper and deeper into their dialogue, that they each were indeed telling the truth. The truth to Job's friends, though, still prevented them from considering the devastating effects upon Job's faith and self-esteem of his ill health, his poverty, his loss of family and friends, and his inability to be at peace with it. Why couldn't they see that? What was blinding them or preventing them from taking it seriously?

The truth to Job, though, likewise prevented him from even considering the possibility that his experience alone was insufficient as a criterion by which one could settle the question of the justice of God. Wouldn't you like to say to Job, *Do you think you are the only one who has ever suffered?* Who would risk saying such a thing to one suffering as Job is? But didn't it need to be said?

Total commitment to honesty about God is almost certainly a lot harder than we think. What if our lies about God are more extensive than we have known? In fact, total commitment to honesty about anything is almost certainly a lot harder than we think.

CARSON

The important thing is not to stop questioning. Curiosity has its own reason for existing. One cannot help but be in awe when he contemplates the mysteries of eternity, of life, of the marvelous structure of reality.

EDMUND BURKE

"So, what if there's no God?" Carson puts a big question on the table. I admit it. I love it when clients put the big questions on the table.

"Good question. What difference would it make to you?"

"It would mean it's stupid to have faith."

"Would it?" I ask, feigning innocence.

Carson is looking for permission to divorce his wife of ten years. He probably wouldn't agree, but that's what I think is going on. They have no kids, and she has apparently been chronically depressed since it became clear, early in their marriage, they were infertile. In our first session, Carson helped me understand how unhappy he is in the marriage. Toward the end of the second session, with no time left to pursue his comment, he'd said that he was wondering about divorce. So that's where I started when we began our third conversation. He'd told me they were active in their church, but he'd not yet put his concerns about religious faith on the table.

"I'm a little bit confused, Carson. Are you asking me to argue for the existence of God, or are you asking if it's OK to get a divorce if there is no God?"

"What? Well...I'm not sure what I'm saying...or asking...."

"Let's see if we can get some clarity. You told me that you had started thinking about divorce. I asked you how that fit within your religion's commitments. You wondered about the existence of God, and whether or not faith makes any sense. I don't know...it sounds like you're trying to find a way to do what you want to do without having the whole God thing mess it up."

"Maybe. I'm not sure. I just know that there would be hell to pay, so to speak, if I brought up the possibility of divorce with Deena. Within twenty-four hours, all of her family and half of mine would be burning up my cell phone. I saw what happened to her cousin. When he left his wife, the fury of her family hit him hard."

"How so?"

"He told me he got five hundred *God hates divorce* text messages from Deena's parents, aunts, and uncles in one day."

"Wow. That's impressive. I guess that's what we get for pushing our parents to learn how to use their cell phones. But this confuses me even more. You started by asking questions about the existence of God, and now it sounds like you're anxious about your wife's family, the existence of which is fairly clear. They seem pretty sure about the mind of God."

"Doesn't the Bible say that God hates divorce?"

"Yes, it does, in so many words. And it always saddens me when people take a verse in scripture and use it like a club without any attempt to understand what a person is dealing with. I figure you must be in tremendous pain if you are willing to even think about divorce, knowing the onslaught you would face. I can see how this would mess with your notions about what it means to have faith. I know you can't completely ignore potential fallout, but can we examine *your* faith?"

"I'm not sure I have any more faith."

"Sure you do. If you scheduled any appointments next week, then you have faith that your car is going start and get you where you need to go. We're 'living by faith' every time we take out a loan. Don't you mean that you've lost faith in your God-story?"

"What's that mean?"

"Faith simply means living as if something is true, even though you can't prove that it is true, hence, the car analogy. You can't prove that your car will start next week, but you live as if your car can be trusted. Religious faith refers to living as if there really is something bigger than us, even though we can't prove the existence of that something. Of course, the fact that there are over ten thousand different religions sort of indicates that humans can't quite agree on exactly what that 'something' is up to, but that doesn't stop a lot of people from insisting they've got it right."

"I'm not sure my in-laws would feel good about me talking to you."

"Maybe not, but they might be surprised that a 'liberal' like me can still give you hell for ignoring your values regardless of what you think about God."

REFLECTIONS

Milton's homily asks some hard questions. If religious faith, at the very least, asks us to be honest, then what does this look like when it comes to what we say about God? Milton asks, *What if our lies about God are more extensive than we have known?*

The homily brought to mind the myriad conversations I've (Wes) had with clients around the question, *What if there is no God?*

What's it like to see that question in print?

What if there is no God?

Do you have any emotional reaction?

Do you have any thoughts about it?

How would your mom or your dad respond if you asked that question? How would your pastor respond?

What if there is no God?

As one who has faith that there is a God, and that Jesus provides us a trustworthy picture of God, I've also come to believe that we will never grasp the wisdom of Job until we can ask ourselves "What if there is no God?" from a place of peace. Otherwise, we are just another one of Job's well-meaning, but frustrating, friends.

I (Milton) would just add that Wes's interpretation of honesty and falsehood about God could venture into questions more difficult than merely whether there is God. The question of what God is like seems equally important and evokes similar motives to be dishonest.

16

PRESSING THE BOUNDARIES OF HUMANNESS

JOB 7:17-18

What are human beings, that you make so much of them, that you set your mind on them, visit them every morning, test them every moment?

CONNECTIONS

Four fundamental questions shape much, if not all, theological conversation:

1. What is God (or Reality) Like?
2. What are healthy human beings like?

3. How do human beings get broken?
4. How do human beings get fixed?

Although the book of Job frequently wrestles with the first question, Milton's homily focuses on how important the other three questions are as well.

Job challenges his friends on their assumptions concerning all four of these questions. Wes challenges Renée to reconsider what it means to be *fixed*.

THE HOMILY

Job's tortured thoughts eventually traverse the mysteries of what it means to be human. When his friend Eliphaz gets philosophical (*Can humans be justified before God...?* [4:17]), Job echoes his words in 7:17 by asking, *What are humans, anyway...?* This sort of skepticism is echoed in Pilate's interrogation of Jesus when he retorts, *What is truth...?* (John 18:38).

Such words tap into the human capability toward bitter irony through rhetorical questions. Nearly all readers know there are no confirmed answers to such questions. But what a marvelous assist for sheer endurance of pain, the kind of verbal sparring that searches for answers by asking unanswerable questions. Questions that are unanswerable diffuse pain by shifting the focus from oneself and the immediate to some other and an indefinite future. Job's question about human worth follows his assertion that he rejects his own life. He will reiterate that later in response to his friend Bildad (9:21). He accuses God of dehumanizing and problematizing him by treating him like the primordial dragon, *tannin* (v. 12). His question in v. 17 seems to reflect genuine perplexity at the purpose of his life. Why would the great creator of the world bother to take human life so seriously as to torture it, Job wonders. There is no pious sentimentality in these words, only the ironclad disappointment of one who thinks his God has turned on him needlessly.

He's not alone in raising such a question, though. The poet of Psalm 8 asks the same thing in nearly the same words: *What are human beings that you are mindful of them...?* (v. 4). Only, in the psalmist's query, the tenor is much different. That poet stands amazed, frankly. He is amazed, first, at the "glory and honor" of being human as a result of God's attention. Second, the psalmist is amazed that this glory is available for all to see by merely looking at God's creation. Those of us for whom things are going well as they were with Job may wonder why Job cannot seem to look at the heavens and see the same thing. "If you'd just look," we say. But those of us who are sitting with Job on the dung heap may alternatively be wondering why the psalmist intones such Pollyannaish words. Can't he see that God allows the most miserable suffering to continue endlessly among his creation?

The poet of Psalm 144 seems a bit more realistic. He recalls the same question, *What are human beings?* (v. 3). Only he notes their ephemerality, *they are like a breath* (v. 4). And the psalmist's words echo those who are at least in trouble, *set me free and rescue me from the mighty waters, from the hand of aliens…* (v. 7).

Who is quoting whom? If you've thought of Job as a man raised in the Hebrew religion, then you might assume his statements are a sarcastic response to the wisdom of Psalms and Proverbs. But it could also be that the psalmists are responding to Job's anguish. Could it be that, like the psalmists, Eliphaz, Bildad, Zophar, and Elihu are trying to respond to Job's anguish in a way that maintains the traditions they hold?

Every time I watch the science channel, I ask Job's question: *What are humans?* Only, for many scientists, it's not a question of what *God* makes of humanity, but of humanity's relationship to the universe. What, in the end, gives this human life its purpose and meaning? How is it possible, in whatever circumstances we find ourselves, to find the answers to our questions? It's the same question the psalmist and the poet of Job were wrangling over; we are just in a new context with new challenges.

RENÉE

> *[The] brain is a machine assembled not to understand itself, but to survive.*

E. O. WILSON

"So, am I your favorite boomerang client?"

I laugh. "Do your kids ask you which of them is *your* favorite?"

"They already know the answer to that one. It's whichever one of them isn't costing me money at the time."

Renée is a joy to spend time with. She first came to see me years ago, after a terrifying yet successful journey through the shadow lands of breast cancer. Renée had endured the shock of diagnosis, the dread of a double mastectomy, and the painful process of breast reconstruction.

After she was declared cancer-free she had descended into a deep depression that caught her, and everyone around her, completely off guard. In my office, she had framed her concerns spiritually. Some of her first words to me those many years ago were, "I've never expected special treatment from God, and I've not been afraid to die. I'm grateful to still be alive, with the prospect of watching my kids grow up. Mike has stuck by my side through thick and thin, and I know I should be filled with joy. Instead, I can hardly pull myself out of bed in the morning, and I find myself writing about death."

A low dose of an antidepressant cleared a bit of that fog, and she began to address her dread with me. Having lived a rather crisis-free life prior to the cancer diagnosis, she had discovered that the faith she carried in her head had not quite soaked down into her soul. She allowed me to sit with her in that dark place as she made peace with how little control any of us actually has in this life. Every couple of years, she returns to my office, always around the anniversary of that diagnosis.

"I always feel like a bit of a failure when I come back here."

"A failure?"

"Shouldn't I be able to handle my life without running to you by now?"

"Gee, Renée. Do you still pay for coaching at the tennis club?"

"Yep."

"Well, you've been playing since you were six years old. Shouldn't you have perfected your game by now?"

"Point taken."

I smile at her. "Seems we always begin your check-ups with this same little dance, and you always say, 'Point taken.' It really is hard to get past the notion that this sort of help is an indication of spiritual immaturity, isn't it?"

"Yes, it is. I was reading my journal a couple of weeks ago and came across an entry I'd made after a conversation we'd had. I'd written, 'Remember: Your brain doesn't care about making sense of things. It just cares about keeping you alive.'"

"That's not a bad paraphrase of the bug-studier's wisdom."

"The what?"

"That quote is from E. O. Wilson. His fascination with all living things began with his study of insects. He concluded that, regardless of our desire to find meaning in life, we're still saddled with a brain that's only concerned with making sure we wake up in the morning."

"And I still sometimes get immobilized by that question, 'Why should I get up this morning?' I still get up. I eat breakfast. I sit down to write. I go visit folks in the nursing home. I touch base with my kids."

"Yeah, so you do meaningful things, even when they don't *feel* meaningful?"

"I guess, and it is helpful to remember that this is at the heart of what it means to live by faith."

"Still, I know it's not easy. When I saw you'd made this appointment, I did an Internet search to see if I could find any of your recent poetry. I was pleased to see how many magazines and websites want your stuff."

"It helps pay the bills."

"I was struck by two of your poems that I came across. In one you are describing the sheer joy of watching a child figure out how the pedals work on a tricycle. You brought me to tears as you reflected on how no one could know what life held for that child, but you were able to share his wonder at his first lesson in physics. How did you put it? Something about how his emerging mind was trying to grasp the same laws that God uses to keep the universe spinning?"

She smiles as she remembers. "Yeah... that was little Joey, my daughter's youngest. I swear I was watching all sorts of circuits come online in his muddled little brain as he figured out how to make that red trike move forward and backward...forward and backward."

"And then I came across another piece you'd done. Was it in *The New Yorker*? You're really hitting the big time. It was haunting and dark. You were describing what it was like to sit with the mother of a dying child. How did you put it? 'What sort of bastard-god conceived of such a universe?'"

"That mother knew I'd come to her side from a birthday party for another of my grandkids. I was determined to be present to her, yet I couldn't escape this sense that she resented me. Probably just a projection on my part."

"Do you recall when you wrote each of those?"

"Seems like they came within a week or two of each other."

"That's amazing. Truly amazing."

"Why do you say that?"

"Renée, you are living the most mature sort of faith. Dysfunctional religion is always trying to explain things, resolve the obvious tensions in life, by offering trite answers. Mature religion helps us to sit in that tension…to find contentment in the paradox."

"I'm not feeling much contentment right now."

"Yeah, I get that. I wonder how much of the discontent is fed by your early religious training that left you believing strong faith always equals perfect peace. All I know is that your poetry challenges a reader to sit with life on its own terms, and I'm grateful for your skill."

"See, this is why I hire you to be my coach. You don't tell me what to think…well…sometimes you tell me what to think. But mostly you have this way of reminding me of what I already know."

REFLECTIONS

I (Wes) was talking to Milton about the myriad problems the book of Job presents to scholars. Milton was explaining how there's virtually no agreement on when the book was actually written, or how it came to be in the form we find in the Bible. I recalled how much I had loved the theory that the central portion of the book is the original story, and that the beginning and ending were later added by sages. The idea is that the rabbis could not stand how messy the story was, so they added an introduction that could lead to an everyone-lives-happily-ever-after ending. I was rather distressed, more recently, when Milt told me that scholars rather tend toward the view that the central part of the story was added later.

I now realize that I liked my original perspective because it supported what I had already decided must be true. We can't stand the messiness of scripture, so we add convenient tidbits to make it go down easier. And then it occurred to me: I'm just trying to create a story about the story that makes me feel better, which is a very subtle small-self strategy. Renée is not succumbing to such a strategy.

17

THE CLASH OF TITANS: EXPERIENCE VS. TRADITION

JOB 8:8-10

For inquire now of bygone generations, and consider what their ancestors have found.

CONNECTIONS

How do you decide what is true? Hardly anyone would deny that the earth revolves around the sun, and not the other way around. Yet Copernicus (sixty some years after his life) and Galileo (during his life) were condemned by the Church for teaching as much. After all, doesn't the Bible clearly say that the sun rises and sets, indicating that it is the sun that is moving, not the earth?

Such interpretations seem ridiculous to modern Christians, yet we still wrestle with the question of when to trust our religious traditions and when to trust what scientists and our personal experiences place before our eyes.

Job is not just clashing with his friends in this book. He is raising important questions about what, and whom, to trust. The conflict raises the possibility that some points of view simply cannot be harmonized, only understood. But what does it mean to live in relationships while holding clashing opinions about important ideas?

THE HOMILY

Epistemology is the study of how we know things. How do we know the sun is hot? How do we know stealing is wrong? I am interested in epistemology because it is concerned with different ways of knowing what is true. I teach it to my students so they can assure their parents that their investment in a college education is sound. Everyone ought to have a word like that to trot out at cocktail parties and church socials. But it's important for other reasons, too. How people know things shapes the meanings they give to their lives. We come to decide how to live our lives on the basis of different authorities deriving from different ways of knowing.

Bildad's epistemology is shaped primarily by his religious tradition. In fact, the appeal to religious tradition is a central feature of what all of the friends are saying to Job. Bildad is the first friend to assert tradition as an authority for understanding Job's plight. He urges: *For inquire now of bygone generations, and consider what their ancestors have found. ... Will they not teach you and tell you and utter words out of their understanding?* (8:8, 10). We would all be lost without the wisdom of those who've gone before us. We all draw relentlessly from the traditions handed down by our culture, our religious training, and our families. Tradition and custom are essential to stability and confidence in the future. No one doubts that.

But Job will have none of it. He baldly challenges the relevance of tradition for understanding his plight: *Is wisdom with the aged, and understanding in length of days?* (12:12). He suggests that his friends are speaking falsely for God, and he argues: *Your maxims are proverbs of ashes, your defenses are defenses of clay* (13:12).

Job acknowledges his friends' points of view, but he challenges them to deeper reflection (12:5a). He insists that his experience has not been fully understood (6:1-3) and that his friends are therefore false to him (6:14). The force of his thinking is that simple observation and reason make it unavoidable that God has wronged Job—why, even nature itself knows it (12:7-10). So Job wants his friends to take his experience more seriously, and his friends want Job to stop undermining the long tradition of wisdom that they all have shared. Who's right on this one?

I began the practice some years ago of taking a daily newspaper for the single purpose of reading the op-ed pages. I was interested in understanding the diversity of the many political and economic opinions that informed so much of the thinking surrounding me. I was not interested in the talk shows on the television, because they offered no time for me to think about what a pundit might have said. Reading something in writing, though, seemed a way to experience the diversity of opinion and have time to ponder it. And, I'll admit, I could follow blogs now, were I not in the habit of reading the paper.

I am filled with wonder at how these political pundits arrive at their opinions. What source of knowledge do they have to arrive at their conclusions so forcefully held? And, in the past fifteen years, there have been some powerful disagreements: from weapons of mass destruction to yet another recovery of the economy and its implications for health care. The issues are endlessly emerging anew.

The problem of *how we know things* stays the same, though. And it is not present in only matters of public policy debates. It affects our religious faith, too. We hold to spiritual traditions we have often called *timeless*. We have been taught that timelessness means that certain values should never change. And then experience happens and forces us to sit and listen to the din of the collision between the two. Timeless wisdom; the values of the moment's crisis. How do we hold these as meaningful authorities for our lives?

REVEREND CRAIN

What Christian faith teaches is never communicated merely by a conceptual indoctrination from without, but is and can basically be experienced through the supernatural grace of God as a reality in us. ...

KARL RAHNER

Dear Dr. Eades,

I recently came across your webpage. I'm wondering why a Christian counselor would quote Buddha and Gandhi.
Rev. Charles Crain

Everything in me tells me to ignore this email. I learned a long time ago how futile it is to engage in impersonal debates with people who are more interested in arguments than relationships. However, I'm also aware that my small self has created an entire story about someone I've never met based on two sentences. I'm assuming that he has done the same to me, based on a couple of quotes on my webpage.

Dear Rev. Crain,

Thank you for your note. I appreciate your question. I suspect that most folks just make their judgments without ever asking for clarification.
I include those quotes for several reasons. My homepage is designed to give readers a quick impression of me. I want people to know that, even though I am Christian, I respect the wisdom I find expressed in other faiths. I want people who are looking for a counselor to understand that I am not someone who will hammer them with Christian orthodoxy. And I also want those who do want a more religiously conservative counselor to know that I'm probably not a good fit.
peace,
Wes

I figured this would be the end of this exchange, though I wasn't all that surprised when another email was waiting for me the next morning.

Dear Dr. Eades,

Do you believe the words of Jesus when he says, "I am the way, the truth, and the light. No one comes to the Father but through me"?
Rev. Charles Crain

Now I *know* I should write a polite response, making it clear that I prefer to not engage in theological debates through email, especially with those who want to correct me. However, again, my small self seems to be looking for a fight.

Dear Rev. Crain,

I do indeed believe those words of Jesus, though I may not own them in the same way you do. As my life has moved along, I've encountered more and more people who seem to have been transformed by commitments to something other than Christianity. I must admit, early on, it was rather unnerving to meet Buddhists whose lives reflected far more of the "fruits of the Spirit" than did mine! LOL
peace,
Wes

Surely this would be the end of it.

Dear Dr. Eades,

I don't think you are a Christian.
Rev. Charles Crain

Why, of all the arrogant…My small self pounds out an angry email, but my Authentic Self restrains me from hitting send. I delete the email, and sit with my anger. If I'm going to correspond with this guy, then I've got to let go of my assumptions…my reactions. I need to honor his honest thoughts, regardless of his motivations.

Dear Rev. Crain,

You're not the first person to suggest I was bound for hell on a Teflon slide. :) However, I'm curious. Even my most theologically conservative friends acknowledge that God is Mystery, and that the

human mind/brain is limited in its ability to grasp God. Do you know how you've come to be convinced that your reading of scripture, and your theological beliefs are the only ones that are accurate? Surely you've met people who don't see God the way you do, yet seem to be living lives very much in sync with the spirit of Jesus.
peace,
Wes

P.S. If you have any interest in continuing this exchange, please call me Wes. Whenever someone calls me Dr. Eades, I look around for my brother, the medical doctor. You know, the kind of doctor that actually helps people! LOL

Well, aren't I proud of myself! I've not taken the bait. I've risen above the fray. I'm so mature!

Dear Wes,

My apologies for the argumentative question regarding your faith. Old habits are hard to break. The truth is, I'm confused right now. To put it in a nutshell, a few years ago my youngest daughter hooked up with some sketchy friends, got into drugs, and angrily denounced Christianity. We kicked her out of the house after we found marijuana in her room, and she literally disappeared until recently. Three weeks ago we get a call from her. She tells us she's been clean for a little over a year. She said she was in a Narcotics Anonymous program, and that it was time to work on her ninth step. She asked if she could meet with us.

When she showed up at the house, I could hardly believe my eyes. I thought about the townspeople running to the cemetery and finding the former demoniac sitting peacefully at the feet of Jesus. We sat down at the table, and she proceeded to lay out all the ways in which she knew she had sinned against us. She apologized for the pain her irresponsibility had inflicted on us, and asked our forgiveness. We almost had to get a beach towel to wipe up the tears.

This is turning into more than a nutshell....Here's where I got thrown. I said, "Honey, Jesus is so proud of you right now." She said, "Daddy, I'm not a Christian anymore. I'm a practicing Buddhist, and it's changed my life."

I'm not very proud of how I responded to her next. Let's just say that most people would have gotten angry and stormed out the front door. She just sat there, calmly, with tears running down her face. She said, "Daddy, I know this is hard for you, but I want us to have a relationship. If we can't, then I'll try to understand."

When she left, all I could think was that my family would be separated for eternity.

I'm not sure why I'm telling you all this.
Charlie

How many different ways am I going to have to learn the lessons I offer to my clients? How often do I ask persons to remember that we're all so deeply wounded? How often do I underscore the need to suspend judgment? Yet here I was getting all worked up over some misperceived confrontation of my faith.

Dear Charlie,

I've just finished reading your email…for the third time. I'm sitting here in silence, feeling like I'm on holy ground. Your pain is so intense, and so honest.

What I can tell you right now is that I've sat with more young men and women like your daughter than I can count. So many people have been scarred by a religious upbringing that they perceived, rightly or wrongly, is more about keeping rules than becoming a loving person. It's not uncommon for such persons to reject the faith of their childhoods, only to find an outlet in another direction.

How can we parents not be troubled by such developments? You are committed to an expression of Christianity that is very clear about who's in and who's out. Your daughter is clearly with the outs. So, are you supposed to just change your theology because it's now become inconvenient? That certainly doesn't seem right, and you strike me as a man of more integrity than that. Yet, is it unreasonable to assume that perhaps there are ways for persons to be "in the Kingdom" and not know it? C.S. Lewis, a hero of evangelicals, certainly thought so. And Karl Rahner promoted the notion of "anonymous Christians."

May I offer a word of advice? (I'll understand if your answer is "no," but you might want to stop reading!) The Jesus I encounter in the Gospels expresses his deepest contempt toward those who elevate rules over relationships. If your daughter decides that you are more concerned about theology than her, then she is going to miss out on the richness of your love for her. I hope you can reach out to her and invite her to help you understand better where her peace comes from.

As much as you and I might disagree on the details of what it means to be a Christian, I suspect we both would affirm that God is in Christ reconciling the world back to himself. Might it be that some aspects of God's redemptive movement through Christ are impossible for us to understand?

peace,

Wes (fellow struggler, and oft-frustrated Dad)

REFLECTIONS

Job's suffering brings him to question his traditional values. Reverend Crain's suffering, resulting from his daughter's newfound spirituality, causes him to cling more tightly to his traditions. Why would that be?

How does suffering impact your relationship to your faith? How do you decide when a point of theology is worth losing a relationship over? Some readers are almost certainly estranged from a family member who has "come out of the closet," while others have faced the same circumstances by shifting their beliefs concerning homosexuality.

Perhaps in Charlie's case we can hear the echo of the satan's words, *Skin for skin! All that people have they will give to save their lives…* (2:4)

Is it that Charlie just hasn't been pushed far enough yet? Or is he truly a man of religious integrity who is not going to shift his beliefs to make life easier to bear?

18

Hope's Endurance...

Job 13:15

See, he will kill me; I have no hope; but I will defend my ways to his face.

Connections

Do you ever consider the reality of your own coming death? Since we are often speaking of assumptions in this book, are you aware of the assumptions you carry about your death? It is very likely that you abide at least a few thoughts about what would make your death *acceptable.*

Job has concluded that he is going to die, and his death will not be *fair*. The homily explores how the prospect of death can reveal much about a person. The counselor's conversation with Nolan explores how our assumptions can lead to bitterness.

THE HOMILY

I think the only verse from the book of Job I ever heard my mother quote was Job 13:15. I wonder why she was so interested in it. I'm sure it was a memory verse from her Sunday school teacher, Mr. F. Paul Horn. The verse is marked in her old King James Bible, which she always told me was a gift from Mr. Horn in 1936 to members of his class. Mom was seventeen when she received the Bible. The verse reads: *Though he slay me, yet will I trust in him: but I will maintain mine own ways before him*. And if to her dying day she ever thought of the book of Job, I suspect that's what she thought it was about: *Though he slay me, yet will I trust in him....*

It's not difficult for Christian persons to hear echoing in such a triumphant acclamation the words of Jesus in his Gethsemane prayer of submission and trust: *O my Father, if this cup may not pass away from me, except I drink it, thy will be done* (Matthew 26:42, KJV). And yet this famous passage from Job may not say that at all. It is entirely possible, and even likely, that the words in this verse are better rendered: *See, he's going to kill me; I have no hope; but I will defend my ways to his face*.

Yes, this chasm of difference in meaning turns on the variation between what was written (*Ketib*, in Aramaic) versus what was read (*Qere*, in Aramaic). And what was *read* made the verse sound like an extraordinary declaration of trust in the face of indescribable suffering and pain.

What has made readers favor one over the other? Of course, you probably don't have the ability to read the ancient languages and are in a bind here, to a degree. Still, it may actually be context that tips the scales one way or another. The poet of Lamentations 3:1-18 offers thoughts that align closely with Job 13:15 when he writes: *Gone is my glory and all that I hoped for from the Lord.* Yet in the context of Lamentations there *is* a reversal that depicts the sufferer as finding some reason to maintain trust: *The steadfast love of the Lord never ceases, his mercies never come to an end* (3:22).

Is it possible, then, to read Job 13:15 as anticipating some kind of deliverance from the all-powerful God, and thus read the verse as an expression of undying trust? In the context of Job's story, just about everything Job has said to this point makes it very dangerous to get too close to God. Job does not see his power affirmatively (see Job 10:3, 8, 14, 15.). Yet Job's friends think that God's power is positive and good. They urge him to see things this way, also.

To read the verse the way it was *written* in antiquity, rather than the way it came to be *read* by those who passed it on, is another matter. Job has every reason up to this point in the story to believe that God *is* going to kill him and that indeed he has no hope of avoiding such a death. And it seems that here Job is finally realizing his mortal fate. And yet, even though his life is about to be over, he must somehow take measures into his own hands to defend his integrity before God. Oddly, he has already lamented that such a defense is hopeless (10:15) and that his days are in fact few (10:20).

So, what does Job want? Why all of this defense of integrity, this yearning for justice, when he already suspects that God is not bound by principles of justice? At least when Jesus submits to the strong likelihood of his own death, he's not holding out false hope that he will be suddenly delivered. And I cannot read that Gethsemane scene believing that Jesus might have had any inkling of an individual resurrection before the *day* of resurrection. The faith of Jesus only makes sense if he thought, *this is it; whatever happens is in God's hands now.* And, on the strength of such surrender of hope, hope may have been liberated and found.

NOLAN

The greatest and most important problems of life are all fundamentally insoluble. They can never be solved but only outgrown.

CARL JUNG

"Well, like my old Sunday school teacher used to say, 'If the King James Version was good enough for Jesus and Paul, then it's good enough for me.'"

"Nolan, did you and I have the same fifth-grade Sunday school teacher?"

Nolan is such a likable guy. Most folks would not expect him to be sitting in a counselor's office, but most folks don't share his curiosity about philosophy and theology. He'd attended a book study I'd done related to spiritual growth, and called me a few weeks after the study had ended. He was always good for a laugh or two when the study group met, but he also asked the sort of piercing questions that suggested a soul in turmoil. In the safety of my office, he's let me in on more of that turmoil. Unknowingly, he has also tapped into mine. Nolan and I are the same age, and, to borrow a phrase from Harry Stack Sullivan, we are more alike than otherwise.

"So, Nolan, how'd your little experiment go?"

He looks a bit sheepish, like a little boy who hasn't done his homework. But he has a copy of Rohr's *Falling Upward*, and I can tell the open pages have already been well worked.

"Oh, I did fine for about three days, at least on the drinking part, but then I discovered that this stuff went down a little better with a bit of *Jack*. I must admit, though, the book has me thinking."

I grimace on the inside. Nolan had told me he was drinking too much. He says it helps him relax in the evening. I'm aware that I tell myself the same thing. His wife insists he just disappears. He doesn't disagree with her, and so he was open to an experiment. A week of no alcohol in the evening, along with at least thirty minutes of spiritual reading. I'd recommended the Rohr book.

"Anything in particular in the book?"

"Well, here's one part that I underlined:"

No Pope, Bible quote, psychological technique, religious formula, book, or guru can do your journey for you. If you try to skip the first journey, you will never see its real necessity and also its limitations; you will never know why this first container must fail you, the wonderful fullness of the second half of the journey, and the relationship between the two. Such is the unreality of many people who "never grow up" or who remain narcissistic into their old age. I am afraid this is not a small number of people in our world today.8

"What about that paragraph speaks to you?"

---

[8] Rohr, Richard. *Falling Upward: A Spirituality for the Two Halves of Life.* San Francisco: Jossey Bass, 2011. Chapter 1

"Reminded me of Dad. He was so bitter by the time he died. He'd become such a bastard, but I'd never thought of him as having never finished growing up, or as being narcissistic. But it fits."

We sit together in silence for a few moments, and then Nolan continues.

"He really was a great dad. He worked night shift when I was little, but he would always get off work, make us breakfast, and take us to school. By the time I was in junior high, he'd made his way into upper management. We lived in a great house and took vacations every summer. He would play with us in the pool for hours, and he was always up for an ice cream run."

"What changed?"

"Shortly after I got out of college and was working my first job, there was some kind of shake-up at his company. Dad retired. I finally figured out that the retirement was not his idea. He had plenty of money, but he seemed really upset by the whole thing. We were sitting in our favorite pub one evening, and I can remember saying to him, 'What the hell, Dad? You've got it made now. You and mom are free to do whatever you want.' He replied, 'Son, don't ever kid yourself into thinking you have any control. You can give your whole damn life to something, and it doesn't matter one bit.' I didn't understand him at all."

"But maybe you're starting to?"

"Yeah."

"What do you suppose you are figuring out now?"

Nolan laughs. "On my way over here, I saw one of those bumper stickers: *Life's a bitch, and then you die.*"

"Like you didn't already know that?" I'm smiling. "Really, how are you thinking about your dad's words now?"

"I'm thinking that I might be in greater danger of becoming my dad than I ever realized."

"Yeah?"

"Why shouldn't I be the happiest guy in the world right now? The kids are all launched and doing well. My business is growing despite the economy. Shoot, my wife even still pursues me for sex!"

"Oh, my God, are you telling me that great sex really isn't the answer?"

"Hey, I'm not complaining…at least not about that. But at a time when I ought to be enjoying the fruits of my labors, I…I…"

"Walk around in a lead overcoat?"

"Yep. That's how I feel."

"I can see how Rohr's book might strike a chord. To paraphrase Joseph Campbell, we spent the first half of our lives climbing the ladder, only to discover there's nothing we want at the top. The fact that you're willing to look at this now probably means you won't become your dad."

"I guess that's a relief…sort of."

"Nolan, I'm thinking about that line from Job that may be the most mistranslated verse in the Bible, 'Though he slay, yet will I trust in him.'" (Job 13:15, KJV)

"That's a mistranslation?"

"Yeah. Actually Job was saying something like, *Well, God is going to kill me anyway, so what's the point?*"

"Life's a bitch, and then you die?"

"Something like that…actually, a lot like that. Nolan, we've touched on the small self and Authentic Self stuff, but this is a place where the concept really gets meaningful. We've always got two sets of values at work. Our Authentic Self values are shaped a lot by our religious training…by all those messages about what we are supposed to be like. But the small self is always looking for ways to get what it wants. It's like having a Garmin that's broken. You keep programming the thing to get you to a museum where you can enrich your mind, but the Garmin keeps trying to get you to Disneyland. You leave the house intending to buy healthy groceries, and find yourself standing in line at McDonald's, saying, 'Supersize, please.'"

"Burger King."

"What?"

"I'm a BK guy." Nolan chuckles. "But I think I get what you are saying. My dad was great at the first half of life stuff, but when the rules started to change, he wasn't prepared."

"That's a dead-on summary, in my humble opinion."

"So, what do I do?"

"You're already doing it, just not in a very conscious way yet. I'd say that your heaviness is letting you know the values and motivations that have gotten you this far in life are not going to get you the rest of way. In some ways, you may be deciding whether or not you really want to be a Christian."

"Whoa. That's rather heavy." Nolan seems genuinely troubled by my remark.

"Think about it. Christian faith asks us to trust that God is moving this broken creation toward a redemptive end. We're asked to trust that sacrificial love is our way of participating, and that we should have no expectations beyond that. Do you think your Authentic Self has really gotten your small self onboard with that trip?"

"Wasn't there some military guy who radioed to headquarters, 'We're completely surrounded by the enemy, sir. We've got them right where we want them.'"

"Wow. I've heard that before. We should find out if that's a true story, because it sure captures what it means to live fully in this life."

REFLECTIONS

Milton: Wes, when I first read this narrative, I found it almost laughable that you were pairing Job's anger about death at the hands of God with the idea of embracing a life ethic of sacrificial love.

Wes: Laughable?

Milton: Well, yes…laughable. I mean, what is sacrificial love, anyway? What does it have to do with a person coming to grips with the inevitability of his own death? Who's doing the sacrificing and who's encouraging it? I found myself wondering if Nolan just needed some medication. He's obviously self-medicating…

Wes: Gawd, you can make me nuts. It seems to you that I'm avoiding the obvious? That Nolan is a good ol' garden-variety alcoholic?

Milton: Yeah, I guess so. To me, sometimes it looks like a guy is in the middle of a heart attack, and you're asking him why he doesn't cut back on fried foods. I *do* trust that you know what you're doing, but how do you know when to address something like alcohol use head-on, and when to set it to the side? And is the concept of *sacrificial love* really the most relevant place to go?

Wes: You're making good points. Sometimes I do take a stance of, "We're not going to get anywhere until we address *this* first." But other times my gut tells me a person like Nolan needs a different kind of conversation.

Milton: And, Wes, you do say that Nolan's alcohol use is something you can relate to. Surely you wouldn't fail to address it more directly with him because you don't want to address it more directly with yourself, would you?

Wes: You've gone from preachin' to meddlin'. And you may be on to something. I'll need to sit with that some more. However, it doesn't challenge my fundamental beliefs that any impulse to avoid sitting in our lives as presented reflects a challenge to our basic assumptions about what it means to live a full life.

19

A Mortal, Born of Woman

Job 14:1-2

A mortal, born of woman, few of days and full of trouble, comes up like a flower and withers, flees like a shadow and does not last.

Connections

Ever notice how many religious folk think a lot about the life after this one? The text behind the homily occurs in a part of the story that reflects upon life's impermanence. But it ultimately rejects any notion of another life beyond this one. Readers, especially Christian readers, may be surprised to see that Job's hope for healing of his situation rests only in this life.

In the counseling session below, Claire and Cooper actualize the immediacy of this life rather than some future life in a rather everyday process of decision-making. What would it be like to live in the now, rather than the not-yet, and to have things go one's way?

THE HOMILY

Job's appeal to mothers is not sentimental here, but rather a way of expressing human moral weakness. But when I read these lines: *A mortal, born of woman, few of days and full of trouble…* (14:1-2), I hear the opening lines of Pergolesi's *Stabat Mater*, "The grieving mother stood weeping beside the cross where her Son was…"

This hymn was probably written in the thirteenth century as a depiction of the suffering of Mary, standing at the foot of the cross, watching her son, Jesus, suffer and die. Pergolesi's treatment opens with a doleful duet between soprano and alto voices, with a series of suspensions that convey the slow and painful decay of life in the agony of both son and mother. Moms always get stuck with the dirty jobs: bringing their children into the world, standing by them as they go out, then bearing the insult of being assigned the symbolism of moral weakness.

Giovanni Battista Pergolesi's own life (1710–1736) seems emblematic of Job's assertion of humanity's brevity on earth: *it comes up like a flower and withers, flees like a shadow and does not last* (v. 2). The composer's twenty-six years seem all the more brief when we discover that he was probably lame in one leg due to polio. In fact, his Italian family was well acquainted with life's brevity through the loss of several children. Pergolesi's own mother died when he was seventeen. And yet, he is known as one of the most important fathers of Italian comic opera. The critics say his musical drama abandoned the heroic themes of the classics and focused instead upon more everyday topics with comedic, not tragic, conclusions.

The danger of speaking of comedy today is that we mistake it for humor and think of wisecracking comedians on the radio stations. That's not what is meant here, though. Jesus' own story is comedic even though it features at its center the darkest of injustices and suffering. The plot begins with the rejoicing of the coming of the Messiah; it turns downward as Jesus draws near to Jerusalem and suffers persecution and death; and then it turns upward with God's resurrection of the Messiah from the grave.

Comedy, in its more conventional meaning, refers to a plotline that leads to a hopeful conclusion. Francesco Degrada wrote, "Pergolesi reveals his idea of religion as an extreme humanization of the sacred."[9] That can only mean that what is considered sacred only makes sense if we come to appreciate it through the everyday lives of people, including their suffering.

I don't think it is accurate to say that Job's view of humanity anticipates an upturned, comedic plot, though. We would like to believe that, I think, especially Christians who have the idea in mind that everything always works out for the best. From what vantage point, though, is one to determine what is best? Job is certain that, if humanity is rendered unclean by virtue of its birth from woman, it cannot be made clean (v. 4). He asserts that while a renewal of life might be possible for a tree, it is not so for humanity (v. 10). And though he imagines that living again after death might actually benefit his case against God (vv. 14-17), he's quite certain that another life after this one of suffering is not possible (vv. 18-19). If anything hopeful is to happen to Job, it must happen in this life. This life is all there is.

Speaking from a Christian viewpoint, there is something wonderfully refreshing about Job's perspective. It means that life here and now is what humanity has been given. What hope there is from God must be found as we come to humanize the sacred. Or, to put it differently, we find our hope as we come to see the sacred in the finite minutia of the everyday human life.

CLAIRE AND COOPER

When one's expectations are reduced to zero, one really appreciates everything one does have.

STEPHEN HAWKING

---

[9] http://www.fondazionepergolesispontini.com/fps/index.php?option=com_content& view=article&id=58&Itemid=319&lang=en Viewed 12.18.12.

"I don't see me giving in on this. I can't believe she's even considering it."

Cooper is glaring at Claire. This is our first conversation, and they've explained the dilemma that has brought them to my office. Claire was recently contacted by a rather prestigious university in the South about a position that fit her description of a dream job. The vice president told her that he was very impressed by what she'd accomplished in her current job, and they wanted her for the position. There is a fly in the ointment. Their four-year-old son has significant respiratory issues, and the university is located in an area almost universally recognized as one of the worst places in the country for allergies. The boy's doctor was terse: "I can't possibly recommend it."

Cooper continues, "I knew when I married her that she was smart and ambitious. When she decided she wanted a child, I was glad to become a stay-at-home dad so that Heath wouldn't be raised by others. I've been glad to take a backseat to her opportunities, and she earns twice as much money as I ever could. But now we're talking about the well-being of our son. I can't believe she is this selfish."

I say, "Claire, I'm still not sure how you are seeing the situation and what you make of Cooper's summary. 'Selfish' must be a hard word to hear. What are you thinking? What are you feeling?"

"I'm not sure. I'm angry. I'm so angry." Claire turns to Cooper, "Selfish? Really?"

"You said you'd call the guy and turn down the job. You still haven't called him! God, Claire, I'm still half expecting you to tell me to pack up because the moving vans will be here next week! You want our son to spend the next few years wearing an oxygen mask?"

I'm getting the idea that Cooper doesn't express assertiveness often. It's a tool he wields awkwardly. He comes off like a guy going after a fly with a sledgehammer.

"Cooper, let me see if I can help Claire unpack her thoughts a bit more. Claire, I get the idea that you've almost always been able to achieve whatever you set your sights on."

"I guess." Claire seems caught between a smile and a glare.

"Can you tell me about another time in your life when you've had to say 'no' to an opportunity?"

"Not really." Now it's definitely a grimace.

Again, Cooper can't contain himself. "Of course not. Even when we had to choose between moving to Ohio so I could do graduate work or her accepting the position here, we both knew we were going to be coming here. Right?" He's challenging her like a lawyer with a witness on the ropes.

I'm wondering if I'll need to ask Cooper to step out of the room for a few minutes. "Claire, I can see that you are completely tied up in knots here. Cooper is framing this as a choice between your career and the well-being of your son. Do you think that's a fair way to describe this dilemma?"

"Yes! Of course it is!" Claire seems more surprised by the force of her response than either Cooper or me. "I'm freakin' *Mommie Dearest*. What kind of mother even considers doing this to her son?"

"Well, I suppose Snow White's step-mom wouldn't hesitate, but I hope you'll understand if I'm not ready to decide that you are evil. Am I giving you too much credit?"

"I'm sure Cooper thinks so." Claire starts to reach toward Cooper, but stops herself.

"This is new territory for Cooper also. I'm thinking that you've always managed to be very clear about your goals and to work hard to achieve them. Wouldn't a lot of people say you've lived a charmed life?"

"I even got pregnant the first time."

"What? You got pregnant the first time you tried? I'm thinking about how none of my three kids were created on the first try…

"I'm pretty sure that I conceived Heath on the very night I told Cooper to toss out the condoms…I was ready to make a baby. Everything goes my way."

"OK. So all those sermons about accepting life on its own terms seem odd to you?"

"Mostly irrelevant."

"Are you willing to explore how the idea of acceptance might be relevant now?"

Claire turns to Cooper. "I'll call the guy tonight. I'll officially turn down the job. Could you at least *pretend* you understand how hard this is for me?"

Cooper is speechless. I'm thinking that he is so unaccustomed to *winning* that he doesn't know how to respond.

I turn to him. "Cooper, I don't know why it is that some people get so far into life before real disappointment smacks them in the face. Most of us get to practice being disappointed along the way. I can see that you don't understand Claire's pain in this situation. Can you choose to be curious with her rather than judgmental of her?"

"I suppose, but right now I feel like the biggest ass in the universe."

"How about you direct curiosity, rather than judgment, toward yourself, as well? My impression is that you both are doing some important soul work. You've been wonderful partners along the way. This situation does not have to turn you into enemies."

REFLECTIONS

I (Milton) find myself imagining how couples like Claire and Cooper get so far down the road without having the sort of confrontation we read above. One thing that comes to mind is that individuals fool themselves with regard to what constitutes real choices. I find myself imagining some of those decisions that Claire and Cooper had made earlier under the pretense of setting out two competing choices. Cooper even admits in one instance that while they were pretending to have options, they both knew in advance which option would be taken. Foreknowledge of the future is like the elimination of real choices in the present. At least, it has to skew the choices that are made in the present.

I think that is why I like the poet of Job's ultimate elimination of some notion of life after this life. Like any one of us, he does not know what awaits on the other side of death. He is only echoing the contemporary view of his culture. But having to deal with reality in the here and now without the possibly false hope of some future remediation gives life an urgency it may not otherwise have.

20.

HOW MUCH LESS A MORTAL

JOB 25:5-6

If even the moon is not bright and the stars are not pure in his sight, how much less a mortal, who is a maggot, and a human being, who is a worm!

CONNECTIONS

When do we cross the line between authentic humility and self-rejection? The writer of the New Testament book of Hebrews declares that we humans are only a little less than the angels (Hebrews 2:7; Psalm 8:5), while Bildad suggests otherwise.

Job's friend Bildad resorts to an extreme viewpoint that ultimately robs humanity of any innate moral worth. His language, obviously used for its rhetorical force, taken literally, eliminates any possibility of real relationship with the human creator.

What if a person's faith, though, turns upon his or her own mental illness? These reflections are inspired by the question of how mental wholeness contributes to what it means to be human and thus what it means to be *saved*.

THE HOMILY

I imagine Bildad rethinking his words after he went home. After all, haven't we all thought that one ought not to be held accountable for what he says in the heat of theological debate? There ought to be a special grace for such situations. The rhetoric used in such exchanges is possibly not necessarily what one actually believes. The rhetoric of conflict, we all know, is extreme. It has to be in order to win the debate. Who would ever expect one to live by such extreme language used in the context of competing argument?

I raise that point because in this very brief chapter, Bildad takes an extreme position on the general moral impurity of humanity. It's difficult to believe that anyone could really believe this, even though we have already heard a less extreme form of it from Eliphaz (4:17-19). Bildad says to Job, *If even the moon is not bright and the stars are not pure in his sight, how much less a mortal, who is a maggot, and a human being, who is a worm!* Human inferiority to God is evidence of their inherent moral impurity.

A friend once gave me a two-minute (*quick and dirty*) explanation of the Reformed notion of human depravity. I remember the explanation, because it came from her as though it were simply a statement from the most authoritative sources. Such sources were never to be questioned. She clarified two aspects of its meaning, as I recall. First, depravity is a result of *original sin* (Augustine mostly gets saddled with this) and describes the human incapacity to choose to love God. Unless God were to intervene, she went on to clarify, humans would never love and serve God on their own.

Second, humans do not always choose what is evil; but when they do choose what is good, that good is affected by their selfish, depraved nature. Thus, even a good thing is tainted by human selfishness. I thought it was a very clever argument, perfect for people who were in need of explanations (like Job?) for the existence of evil under the rule of an allegedly good God.

I also remember thinking such a notion of human depravity was quite comprehensive. If one accepts it, there is really nothing inherently good about humans at all. And while I do not think that Bildad's speech in these verses is nearly so thoroughly conceived as the much later notion of human depravity, it is at least as extreme. For Bildad, humans are maggots and worms. And in the biblical story, these creatures signify death and the grave (17:14; 1:26; Isaiah 14:11).

So, the image appeals to the ultimate end of humanity, which is death. And death as the end of all humans becomes a basis for arguing that humans lack moral worth. And yet, does Bildad's view go as far as the Reformed Christian view that says humans cannot even choose to do good unless God equips them to do so? For Bildad, humans may be more like maggots and worms in God's presence, but it does not venture so far as to conclude that humans cannot choose good.

Nevertheless, such positions seem a high price to pay for the comfort that comes from religious faith in God, don't they? I mean, does one really have to accept the extreme position that Bildad sets out in order to find meaning in one's faith? Doesn't the idea of depravity in itself offer a strange comment upon the claim in Genesis 1 that God saw that everything was good? Yes, I know; that occurs in the biblical story before the so-called *fall*. But can we really accept the far-fetched notion that everything ceased to be good once humanity was banished from the garden (the actual reason given is that they might *reach out his hand and take also from the tree of life, and eat, and live forever*... Genesis 3:22)? I just think that when he returned home, Bildad was hoping no one but Job and a loving God were listening to what he said.

Marianne

> *I thought of the voices as...something a little different from aliens. I thought of them more like angels...It's really my subconscious talking, it was really that...I know that now.*

John Nash

"She was back last night. She was sitting right there on the end of my bed. I know she's not *real*."

"But it's still scary?"

"I guess so…a little bit. I just never know what to do with her rantings. I seem to be five years old all over again, listening to momma tell me I'm going to hell."

What picture comes to mind when you hear the phrase *earth mother*? For me, it's Marianne. She's in her mid-fifties with long, gray hair that she wears in a loose braid. Always dressed in billowing, cotton clothing, she could be a character in Little House on the Prairie. But Marianne is particularly unique. She wrestles with a severe thought disorder, and she knows it. Think John Nash in *A Beautiful Mind*. She was diagnosed with schizophrenia as a young adult, and inflicted a lot of pain on herself before she acknowledged her need for help. Other therapists and doctors had helped her come to terms with her challenges. She was referred to me because of the religious content of her hallucinations.

"Tell me more."

"Well…I find it much easier now to accept that she's a personification of my fear. And when she tells me I must draw blood to cleanse myself, I don't feel a need to go searching for the Exacto knife." Marianne is very *matter of fact* as she reports her thoughts.

"I've been concerned that our conversations might really stir up your wounds. You do an amazing job of sitting with the anxiety, of using the skills you've learned."

"Yeah. I can be OK with momma showing up, and if she never goes away, I can live with that. I know I don't have to do what she tells me to do, or believe what she tells me to believe."

"Last week you said that there was something about how we were talking about God, and grace, that was really piercing something in you."

"Oh yeah. No doubt. That's what momma was raving about last night. How did she put it…*You think God has forgiven you? You think you can sleep well at night? God rained down fire on the prophets of Baal, and you can bet he's coming for you!*" Again, Marianne is surprisingly calm as she describes this unsettling scene.

"Yikes! Didn't you tell me that was one of the Bible stories she used to read to you at bedtime?"

"Yeah, if she was sober enough." She smiles. "Anyway, I think I know why she made an appearance. I've been reading *The Shack*. Last night I read the part where Mack tells Jesus that he feels lost. And Jesus says something to him, like, *I'm sorry you feel so lost, but I* am *with you.* And then Jesus underlines it, *You are* not *lost*."

"Powerful words?"

"Yeah, but I've read stuff like that for years. Last night, though, something in me said, *Marianne, you finally believe me, don't you?* And I thought, *I think I actually do.* I drifted off to sleep sort of marinating in that. Then momma showed up, all decked out in that same blue dress she wore to church every Sunday."

"The broken parts of our minds can sure remember the details."

"Why does she…I mean…why do I have such a need to intimidate myself? What is it in me that is so afraid to shift how I think about God and God's grace?"

"Oh, I can come up with a good theory to answer that *why* question, but who knows if it would be true. I'm pretty sure, though, that for most of human history, groups have used dysfunctional religious ideas to try and maintain cohesion. If someone starts raising questions about beliefs, things can get nasty quickly. It takes a brave man or woman to ask, *But what if we're wrong about God?*"

"That makes sense, but what do I do about it?"

"It seems to me that you already are doing something about it. You are exploring your faith and spirituality. And when your anxiety pops up, you don't react to it. You sit with it. I don't know why some people get a *Damascus Road* sort of transformation. I just know that most of us have to muddle along like Peter."

"She's here, you know." Marianne is smiling.

"What do you mean?" I'm sure I look a bit startled.

"Momma's here. I noticed her standing over there in the corner a few minutes ago."

It takes every bit of concentration I can muster *not* to glance at the corner Marianne is nodding toward.

"Really? What do you suppose that means?"

"She's glaring at you, but she's keeping her mouth shut."

"You seem very calm right now."

She smiles broadly. "Indeed, I am. Momma, I know it's not a good idea for me to speak to you as though you are real, but I want you to know that you are welcome in here any time you want to show up."

"I think I believe you."

"What do you mean?"

"You are not lost."

REFLECTIONS

Milton: You know, Wes, mental illness is something I wish theologians talked about more. So much of a theological perspective rests upon some shared assumptions about what is real and how we know it. And I find that persons' emotional states can change such notions of reality.

Wes: That's true. Mental illness can be a blurry concept. We find it easy to judge a woman's mental health when she literally sees the physical presence of her dead mother. But what about when you hear the tepid compliment of your sermon as a ringing endorsement of your preaching skills? Both reflect disconnections from *reality*.

Milton: Funny. But what about when a person's mental state renders her unable to participate within the boundaries assumed by the long-standing doctrines of religious faith? I guess I am wondering how that changes your understanding of those accepted boundaries. Is religious faith just for people with certain mental capabilities?

Wes: I wonder if you're bumping up against one explanation of why there are so many different brands of Christianity (and of Judaism, Islam, Hinduism, and Buddhism, for that matter). A person who experiences ecstatic visions and is convinced of miraculous healings is going to feel much more at home with our Pentecostal brethren than in a traditional Episcopal setting, but that's not really the question you are raising. If I'm going to believe that meaningful religious practice is not limited to only those with advanced education, then I've got to believe it's not limited to those with *good mental health*, whatever that means.

Milton: So how *do* you think about the religious faith of the Mariannes you've worked with over the years?

Wes: I suppose my approach has been shaped by the encounter between Jesus and the demon-possessed man.[10] On many levels, this is a very confusing story for me, but it offers a stark picture of two key features of mental illness: isolation and self-destruction. The story begins with the poor soul consumed by both. For as long as I've been studying psychology and spirituality, it has been a commonly held assumption that isolation and self-destruction are key elements of an unhealthy mind.

Milton: So you'd be more concerned about whether or not Marianne believes what her dead mother says to her than her perception that Mom is present?

Wes: Yeah. That's not to say that I don't think it matters that Marianne literally *sees* her mother, but almost all of the clients I've ever had who deal with such things have received lots of medical treatment, often with limited results. On the other hand, I've worked with some people whose terrifying delusions disappeared when they've taken an atypical antipsychotic. What I want people to trust is that one doesn't have to remain immobilized even when the medications don't bring relief.

---

[10]   Matthew 8:28-34; Mark 5:1-10; Luke 8:26-39

21

GOD'S DISCIPLINE

JOB 5:17

How happy is the one whom God reproves; therefore do not despise the discipline of the Almighty.

CONNECTIONS

Ever heard the old saw that suffering is God's way of teaching us? What do you think about this? Teaching assumes intention. Does God intentionally inflict suffering in order to teach us? This homily explores this tradition that seems to crop up everywhere.

In the counseling session Tom reveals that he stopped going to worship because such statements seemed so utterly backward to him. He would never take seriously a homily from Eliphaz. It takes a referral to a pastoral counselor to surface in both Tom and Emma the feelings that they both instinctively have about God, and how these feelings affect the anger in their relationship.

THE HOMILY

I've always been bothered by the idea that suffering is God's way of disciplining someone. I think Job is, too. The music throughout the film *Lorenzo's Oil* (1992) may subtly remind us of such objections. The *Ave verum corpus*, "Hail, true body," is a hymn that originates from a poem written in the fourteenth century. Its language celebrates the elevation of the host in the Roman Catholic Eucharistic service. I only know it musically from Mozart's setting, although I have been told there are other worthy settings. It is a prayer that Christ's body will be a foretaste of the healing and wholeness of heaven as the partaker faces his own death. It was an especially poignant presence played throughout the film *Lorenzo's Oil*.

The film explores the emotional extremes two parents experience as they seek to find someone who will address their son's illness, *adrenoleukodystrophy* (ALD). In the film's conclusion, it is the parents who find some kind of remediation for their son's suffering and inevitable death. It comes through their own research and insistent intrusion into the lives of many other people. As I reflected upon the text of the *Ave verum corpus,* I was not certain how the music was intended to function in the film. And maybe reflecting upon its intent is simply an irrelevant question. Nevertheless, was the *Ave verum corpus* the implicit prayer of the parents in the film? Was it a subtext that somehow all suffering is related to either God's willingness to intervene or not?

As I watched the film, I could not rid my mind of the somewhat buoyant statement of Job's friend, Eliphaz. He dutifully tries to ease Job's pain by saying in his first speech: "How happy is the one whom God reproves; therefore do not despise the discipline of the Almighty" (5:17).

He continues in this context to summarize all of the benefits of submitting to suffering as the discipline of God. But, incidentally, what is immediately so surprising is the recollection of what Eliphaz had already at least implied. He had urged that, due to human worthlessness and inferiority before God, suffering was simply inevitable. Far be it to think that God would even take the time to educate such humans (4:17-25). So, does he really think that suffering is God's way of educating humanity? In fact, how often have we heard people of religious faith say to us that suffering is God's way of getting our attention?

If we view matters of suffering as God's way of teaching us something, we might not like what it says about God. Consider a moment the subsidiary suffering of all others involved in order to get Job educated. What about the suffering of his wife, for instance? She obviously lives on only to bear witness to her husband's pain, enduring the grief of the loss of her children. The Greek version of the story presents her saying to her husband: ...*And I am a wanderer and a servant from place to place and house to house, waiting for the setting of the sun, that I may rest from my pangs which now beset me* (Job 2:9, Septuagint[11]). What a costly way for God to get Job's attention. In fact, what kind of a God would do that? Is God really so diabolical or so shortsighted? Or is this the only way that God *could* communicate with humanity? Is that the God that we people of faith commit to serve? The idea that suffering is God's way of communicating, instructing, or disciplining, just seems theologically too costly. There must be another way of thinking about God's involvement in human suffering without asserting that suffering is God's way of benefiting creation. But what is that other way?

TOM AND EMMA

It is painfully easy to define human beings. They are beings who, for no good reason at all, create their own unnecessary suffering.

NATSUME SŌSEKI

"So, after Emma threw her glass across the room, I decided to throw mine."

---

[11] The word *Septuagint* broadly designates the Greek translation of the Hebrew scriptures, which began to appear in the ancient Jewish world as early as the 3rd century BCE.

"I was shocked," Emma offers. "I'm the one who throws things, not Tom."

"And then?" I ask.

"I asked Emma if she thought we ought to tell you," muttered Tom.

Tom and Emma were referred to me by some of their friends who had come for some marriage help last year. Tom and Emma had married young, when Emma was pregnant, and then she'd lost the baby. Five years later, they still had not been able to have children. The conflict between them had been slowly rising, and they'd made an appointment with me after Emma smashed a serving bowl given to her by her deceased grandmother. This was our third appointment.

"Evidently you agreed to let me in on this episode, but I'm wondering what happened next."

"We went to bed," says Tom.

"That was it? You both got up and went to bed?"

"Well, we cleaned up the glass," Emma adds. "But then we just went to bed."

This description of events arouses my curiosity. "How do you suppose you kept this situation from escalating like the other situations you've told me about?"

"I don't know what Emma was thinking, but I just kept hearing your question in my head, *What kind of man do you intend to be?* And I knew I'd just been a man who throws things when he is angry. If I don't want to be a man who screams and cusses when he's mad, I sure as hell don't want to be the sort of man who throws things."

"I don't know what I was thinking. Tom chucking that glass across the room sort of stunned me."

"I've got rather mixed feelings and thoughts right now," I say. "On the one hand, I'm thinking I should congratulate you on stopping the escalation. But, on the other hand, I'm concerned the two of you reinforced a really sinister rule. A rule something like, 'It's OK to inflict pain in order to be taken seriously.'"

"What do you mean?" asks Emma. "We never hit each other or throw things at each other."

"No, we just scare the hell out of each other." Tom is rolling his eyes.

"That's what it seems like to me, Tom. Emma, it doesn't appear that you are consciously trying to scare Tom when your feelings overwhelm you, but when you react violently, it scares him. Tom, it sounds like, in the past, you've made efforts to control her outbursts, but you've learned that you have to get verbally abusive in order to get anywhere with her."

"Not that it works," Tom replies.

I smile grimly. "Should I be concerned that, after only two appointments with me, you've figured out that throwing things is more effective?"

Emma's attention turns from the window back to me. "This is so stupid. I'm so stupid. I swore I was not going to turn out like my mother."

"Oh, Emma, you are so not your mother," Tom says softly.

"She threw fits all the time when she didn't get her way."

"Emma, how did your dad respond?"

"He would plead with her to settle down. He'd start doing anything that might please her...washing the dishes...offering to buy her something."

Tom adds, "But, Emma, she drank like a fish and was hooked on pain killers. You're nothing like that."

"You're right, Tom. Emma is so different from her mom in so many, many ways. But Emma, you're saying this like it's a new thought."

Emma seems to hear the question behind my statement as she says quietly, "I guess it's sort of a new thought...No, not really...."

Tom starts to speak again, but he sees me subtly raising my hand, asking him to sit quietly.

Emma continues, "Tom, I can't honestly say that I've been completely unaware that I use the same strategies with you that my mom used with my dad. Lord knows you don't respond like he did."

Emma turns inward again, like she's trying to pull together something, then she offers more.

"Wes, it really pissed me off when you told us that most couples don't make much progress until each is willing to declare, *Our conflict is my fault.*"

"Emma, just to make sure we're on the same page, I told you that conflict is almost always very complex. But since our personal reactions are really the only thing we can control, we each have to own our place in the mess before anything can improve. I was making the same statement to Tom. Still, it sure sounds like you are trying to take me seriously."

"But why would I keep returning to such ridiculous behavior?"

"Me too," adds Tom. "Why would I head down the road the way I do when we are fighting?"

"OK," I begin, "I'm having a thought that might be way off base, but I trust you'll tell me whether or not this fits. I'm thinking about how, for many people, especially very religious people, there can be this notion that inflicting pain on someone in order to get his or her attention is somehow a loving thing to do. I know that the two of you are not religious in any traditional sense, but surely you've heard Christians talk about how God causes suffering so we'll learn something."

Tom says, "That sort of thinking is why I stopped going to church as soon as I had a choice. But what's this got to do with us?"

"I'm just aware that many people can't handle a God who is not in control, so they make suffering a part of God's *will*, something that God inflicts intentionally, in order to teach us something. I often wonder if we do the same thing in our relationships. We give ourselves permission to behave in ways that inflict suffering, and we find ways to justify it as for some greater good. I tend to think it's mostly a way to cope with our own anxiety."

Emma asks, "But what would be the greater good for us to treat each other like we do?"

"Well, if my way of thinking about this fits, then the supposed *greater good* would be that it distracts both of you from asking the harder questions."

Now Tom asks, "Harder questions like...?"

"Oh, to paraphrase Thomas à Kempis, 'Why am I so angry that I can't control others when I can't even control myself?'"

"I guess that gets us back to that core question," says Emma. "What kind of person do I want to be?"

"Yeah," I add. "But it can really be hard to let go of all those small-self rules that get in the way."

REFLECTIONS

Milton: Wes, I'm heartened by Tom's rejection of the view of God as inflicting suffering in order to teach lessons. But the harder questions in Job's case seems to be why is he so angry, and why can't he seem to control his anger. How is what you are telling Tom and Emma any different from what Eliphaz is telling Job? It just sounds like a modified take on, *Remember, Job, in difficult situations, your response is the only thing you can change.*

Wes: The core difference, in my opinion, is that Eliphaz is telling Job that he *knows* what God is like, and that Job is misguided in his anger. If Eliphaz didn't feel so threatened by Job's pain, perhaps he could have helped his friend explore his anger rather insisting he put a lid on it.

Milton: OK, that's an important difference. But still, for Job to change himself means he's got to acknowledge that he has been incorrect in his assumptions about God, which were perhaps the assumptions given him by his most sacred traditions. Who would say this to Job?

Wes: Really? You can't imagine me saying that to Job?

Milton: You're right. There's probably nothing you might say that should surprise me. But Job's counselors are his friends. You, I, and most readers of Job decide their counsel is not only ineffective, but they simply offer advice that is wrongheaded. It would be easy to conclude that they'd much rather see Job suffer than question their own traditions.

Wes: So aren't you just pointing out what we've been saying all along? I recall hearing a story about catching monkeys by hollowing out a coconut and drilling a hole in it just big enough for a monkey's hand. You then put a nut in the coconut. A monkey comes along, reaches into the coconut to take the nut, but the hole is too small for the hand to be removed while holding the nut. I'm told lots of monkeys will let themselves get captured rather than let go of the nut and run away.

Milton: Do you really offer those sorts of examples to your clients?

Wes: I just remembered that story…but I bet I'll start using it. Don't you think it brilliantly captures our small-self tendency to give up our birthright for a bowl of porridge?

Milton: Whatever.

22

CRITICAL RELIGION

JOB 12:11

Does not the ear test words as the palate tastes food?

CONNECTIONS

When was the last time you *really* had to trust someone when the stakes were high? As we edit these connections, we are all reeling from the shooting deaths of adults and children at an elementary school in Connecticut. What has it been like for those of you with young children to drop them off at school in the aftermath of such a horrible event? What's it like to *trust* that your children will be safe?

Side by side, the homily and the counseling session seem to explore the impracticability of being critical in all things. By *critical* we mean that approach to life that acts on the basis of reasons.

But it's one thing to test the meanings of words that form our traditions. It's quite another to live in relationship with another person, while living in an unpredictable and dangerous world. I heard someone say about her marriage, "Once trust is gone, the relationship is over." And, we can probably easily see how that could be applied to religious faith, too. And yet, there's Job. And further, there are couples like Sabrina and Keith, trying to work it out.

The Homily

We may not agree with Job's notion of human physiology, but we cannot avoid his critical acuity. Can religious faith be critical? By critical, I don't mean something negative, but rather I refer to decisions that are based upon careful reasoning. Critical thinking involves systematic reflection on our assumptions, and a willingness to change our minds. Critical thinking seems more in line with a twenty-first century textbook on scientific method rather than an ancient story about a suffering man and his faith in God. But Job is the one who indeed says, *Does not the ear test words as the palate tastes food?* as a call for greater discrimination in the use of arguments that come from tradition.

That word *test* is not uncommon throughout the biblical story, either. Job's fourth friend, Elihu, uses the same words to continue his critique of Job and the other friends (34:3). What is more, the writer of Ecclesiastes believes that wisdom itself is a criterion by which one makes such tests, assuming that enough wisdom is available (Ecclesiastes 7:23).

These ancient thinkers do not merely accept blithely their inherited traditions about God. They seem to think that those traditions must be tested. I'm not suggesting that the ancient attitude toward such testing is equivalent to contemporary Western, post-Enlightenment attitudes. In our civilization, practically nothing exists unless it is material and verifiable. However, I think it is helpful for all of us to be interested in exploring how far such a critical attitude might have reached in the ancient world.

There is no question that God does plenty of testing throughout the biblical story. The narrator of one of the most important biblical stories, *the binding of Isaac*, states baldly that God was testing Abraham

(Genesis 22:1). In fact, the poet of Psalm 26 yearns for God to test him that God might see that his motives for service have been pure and unwavering (Psalm 26:2). Evidently the language of the psalm envisions some desperate situation in which death seems imminent and that continued life and health would prove the innocence of the one voicing the prayer.

Nor does God seem to like it much when God is put to the test. Jesus appeals to scripture in the face of his own temptation by the devil (Matthew 4:7) to assert that putting the LORD to the test is simply not to be done. It gets Jesus off the hook, temporarily. The passage Jesus quotes is Deuteronomy 6:16, which appeals to the story in Exodus 17:2, where the people following Moses wanted (needed?) water and Moses scolds them for *testing* the the LORD. Evidently, the highest degree of piety is that of trusting the LORD even when there is a scarcity of one of the most vitally important ingredients for human life: water. (Surely this is an example of what it means to fear God for nothing!)

So maybe this partially explains why the book of Job is not that popular among persons of religious faith. That is, the hero of the book seems to assert the importance of *testing* words to see if they are valid, even traditional words about one's faith in God. And testing God is not really why people of faith embrace faith. Isn't it rather just for the opposite reason that faith is meaningful? In fact, isn't testing God just the opposite of faith? Faith, as contemporary Christians have learned, is about committing to certain convictions and actions in the absence of knowledge. How would one test the claim of the resurrection of Jesus, anyway? A resurrection (not resuscitation) is not exactly something that has ever happened before or since.

It is even more remarkable that Job continues to voice his complaints *toward* God, while wanting to test God, or test his convictions about God. That seems to be a remarkable mix of both faith and criticism, doesn't it? Don't you wonder what that would look like in everyday life?

KEITH

I've smoked a little pack and I've drunk a lotta gin
And I've even been down to a house of sin
The things I've done I can't undo
But if God can forgive me, why can't you?

MAC SLEDGE (ROBERT DUVALL)

"I don't know if I can do this. Every time I think I'm getting somewhere, I see her cell phone sitting there, and I start digging through it, looking for clues."

"You're making yourself a bit crazy?"

"Wes, I may have to end this marriage. I can't live like this."

The phrase *painfully fascinating* goes through my mind at least once a week, and it fits where Keith is right now. He is the injured party in an all-too-common scenario:

Wife goes to fifteenth high school reunion.

Wife runs into old boyfriend.

Wife has one-night stand.

Wife is filled with guilt and remorse.

Wife confesses to husband.

The wife in this story is Sabrina, and I don't think I've ever met a woman who has turned such a poor decision into such personal growth. Her words early on were, *I never imagined I was capable of such a thing, and now that I know I am, I have to own it.* Sabrina teaches fifth-grade Sunday school at their church, and another of her comments was, *I'm not sure we've ever figured out how to talk to kids about sin and grace in ways that make sense to them. I don't think I've ever understood those concepts until now.*

I've been down similar roads with countless couples. I would never recommend an affair as a path to marriage enrichment, but there's no question that many couples point to such a painful experience as the catalyst for genuine growth in their relationships. Such is not the case here. It has been nearly five months since that reunion, and Keith seems as undone as he was the first time I saw them. Today I wanted to meet with him alone.

"What do you suppose you just can't trust about Sabrina's commitment to you?"

"I don't know. I just don't know. She's doing all the right things. She answers every question I ask. She's given me all her passwords. Nothing has happened in the past five months to make me think she isn't genuinely sorry and committed to our marriage."

"But there's really no way to *prove* something like commitment, is there?"

"I don't know if I can do this. How do I know it's not going to happen again?"

"It sure would be comforting if we could come up with a fool-proof test."

"No kidding."

"Keith, you are wanting Sabrina to *fix* your anxiety. There's no question that another person can help us manage our anxiety to a degree, but no one can fix it for us. Sabrina can't prove the authenticity of her commitment to you any more than God can prove his existence to you. You can test her all you want, but it will never be enough. The most genuine sorts of relationships are never based on tests."

"So I'm supposed to suck it up and be miserable?"

"You're not *supposed* to do anything, but you do have choices here. I'd like to help you make those choices based on your deepest values, not on what's going to help you feel better in the moment. You took your marriage vows in church, right?"

"Yeah." Keith seems curious about where I'm going.

"And I assume your vows included all that 'till death do us part' stuff?"

"Sure. We were very traditional."

"And so, were you promising God to hang in there through thick and thin?"

"I suppose."

"OK, so how would you leaving Sabrina reflect any less unfaithfulness than her one-night stand?"

"Really?" Keith's voice is rising. "You're going to say that I'd be just as bad as her for leaving? You're going to bully me with the guilt-and-shame card?"

"Maybe it sounds like that, but I don't believe that's what I'm saying. I think I'm inviting you to step back and frame your pain within the context of the larger Christian story you profess. Scripture is full of all sorts of confusing stories about testing God and demanding proof. Sometimes it seems like God honors such tests, and other times God seems angry about it. To me, this mirrors a dilemma in all close relationships. We want proof, but ultimately we have to decide if we will trust."

"So it's that easy. Just trust that she won't do this to me again?"

"Keith, I know this isn't easy. Faith never is. It seems to me that we rarely figure out just how hard faith can be until it's asked of us in a very personal way. I'm wondering if this isn't really about trusting Sabrina. I'm pretty sure she's gotten her vaccination against affairs and knows she doesn't want to make these sorts of choices again."

"If it's not about trusting her, then what's it about?"

"I suspect it's about dealing with just how impossible it is to create a life that is completely safe and secure. Life has never been safe. You've just never had your nose rubbed in it like this before. I'm not saying that it's wrong to *test* a person's commitment. But you've done that, and it seems to me that Sabrina has passed with flying colors. So, if a test was going to fix you, I think you'd already be fixed."

Reflections

Milton: Wes, I'm really drawn to your approach to Keith. I think I agree with you when you point out to Keith that his issues of trusting Sabrina are more about his own anxiety than her ability to be faithful. It does not discount Sabrina's unfaithfulness. But it does shine a very bright light on the various levels of illness that prevent Keith from reclaiming his trust.

Wes: In this situation, I find it rather easy to head down this path. Like I say, it is clear to me that Sabrina has gotten her *vaccination.* There really are a lot of people who just need one experience like this to realize what a horrible choice has been made. Sometimes, though, I'm not sure at all about the *unfaithful* person. Plenty of times the continued suspicions seem warranted. I'm wondering if Job is in this second group.

Milton: Things really do get complicated when we try to apply this to Job, and to religious faith in general. When a couple gets married, some very clear vows are exchanged. Sabrina would say she clearly broke a promise. She clearly violated Keith's trust.

Wes: Right. But to what degree does this fit Job's situation? Has God violated Job's trust, or has God just not been bounded by Job's assumptions about who God is and how God works? Does it make sense to be angry with God, or a person, for not living up to my illusion?

Milton: So Keith makes assumptions about Sabrina based on what he needs her to be, and Job makes assumptions about God based on who he needs God to be? I get it. Of course, let's cut Keith and Sabrina some slack. Even though they exchange vows at the beginning of their marriage, they cannot know what the boundaries on those vows might be. On the other hand, one of the obvious boundaries, I suppose, is committing adultery, no? Are there as obvious boundaries that simply have to go along with expectations of God? I suppose.

Wes: I guess that's what I'm saying...

Milton: At the end of the day, both Job and Keith are struggling with anxiety over what it means to have faith. I hear you saying that Keith has to recognize that he brings dysfunction into the relationship, as does Sabrina. As far as religious faith can be critical, it must also allow individuals to be critical of themselves as well as gracious to themselves. And that means that in a trusting relationship, whether marriage or religious faith, one operates with a decided lack of knowledge. Am I reading too much into your therapeutic approach?

Wes: Nope. I'd say you are summarizing my approach quite well.

23

I Know that My Redeemer Lives

Job 19:25

I know that my Redeemer lives, and that at the last he will stand upon the earth.

Connections

Have you been guilty of hearing this verse through Handel's oratorio, *Messiah*? Job's triumphant language (as Handel and his librettist, Jennens, read it) takes an unexpected turn when we begin to recognize that the identity of God as redeemer is a real problem. God seems to be causing Job's problems. How can he be the redeemer? And there is probably no way to resolve this question within the story of Job.

In the counseling session, George has figured this out in a very concrete way and has to rethink what it means to have a redeemer of some sort at all.

THE HOMILY

Is Job's notion of a redeemer an expression of his sense of some sort of entitlement? After all, a redeemer was one who intervened on a family member's behalf. Usually it was the nearest relative, but the expectation was that this person had the responsibility of buying back family property (Leviticus 25:25-34). Or a redeemer might buy a relation out of slavery (Leviticus 25:47-54). He might marry a kinsman's widow (Ruth 3:12; 4:1-6). The redeemer was called upon to act as an avenger of the death of a murdered relative (Deuteronomy 19:6, 11-12). The LORD himself was understood as a redeemer for those who were weak and disenfranchised, especially in court (Proverbs 23:11). In fact, as the people of ancient Israel told their religious traditions, they understood the LORD as their near kinsman who intervened as redeemer on their behalf (Exodus 6:6; Psalm 74:2; Isaiah 43:1; 49:7-9). Christianity itself has come to develop as one of its core affirmations the need for a redeemer from sin.

And anyone who has ever been in difficult circumstances due to financial loss or failing health knows how deeply appreciated some timely outside intervention can be. This makes it all the more difficult for me to understand my own grandfather's opposition to President Roosevelt's social security provisions early in the twentieth century. My father used to tell us that it was absolutely off-limits even to say Roosevelt's name in the house. His policies had become loathsome to Pop. Dad disagreed, of course. Yet, there was not much room for disagreement with my grandfather. Dad would laugh as he told the stories, though, creating a kind of ambivalence I did not understand. On the one hand, I could tell that it had been a major source of tension between them. On the other hand, Dad always seemed to understand exactly why Pop held so firmly to that view. Pop was afraid that social security would create a race of weaklings who could not stand up for themselves and who came to expect the government to intervene in every little detail of life. I always wonder whether my grandfather and I could have talked about this verse in Job 19.

The biblical idea of a redeemer rests firmly upon the notion of the strength of family, though. The redeemer is the near kinsman. And perhaps Pop was not disagreeing with the principle but rather the way it was enacted. I could imagine his making the case for a difference between government intervention and family intervention (although cautiously; the family tradition is that he was a man of notoriously few words).

And yet, though I never actually remember my own father having a conversation with him (I was too young when Granddad died), I can also imagine Dad trying to explain how the advance of civilization, its urbanization and industrialization, had contributed to the diminishing of the family and thus of traditional family values. What is more, I know that my father was moved by the horrible poverty and suffering in the great depression of the 1930s. Family values, while important, have to be modified to fit in with the circumstances, he would say. Government has by the will of the governed been forced to take an increasing role in the protection of the weak, the marginalized, and the powerless.

So when Job says he knows his redeemer lives, who is he talking about? It's doubtful it could be a family member. How could a family member win a lawsuit against God? To press further, if it were one of the holy ones, as Eliphaz seems to think Job calls for (5:1), how could an angel resist the will of God? They may be divine, but they are in inferior roles, as is Job himself. It couldn't be God, could it? How could God stand as redeemer to Job against Godself? That just leaves Job, then, doesn't it? If so, Job has to act as his own redeemer. He has to argue his own case that will both bring God to justice and, while Job is still alive, will bring God into Job's presence (19:26b). Such audacity; such stalwart individuality! I think my grandfather would have liked this thought about Job. Yet, aren't we reading the ravings of a madman who is so racked with pain and grief that he is spouting more his wishes rather than his certainty of things? It may well be that we cannot take Job seriously at this point at all.

GEORGE

Belief in God does not exempt us from feelings of abandonment by God.

EUGENE PETERSON

George was referred to me by the employee assistance program at his work. His seventeen-year-old daughter, Shannon, had recently decided she was ready for hospice care. She had fought an unusual form of bone cancer for over a year, but it was clear that treatment had reached the end of the road, and the cancer was winning. George and I spent the first two appointments bringing me up to speed on the story, and sitting together in the darkness of it all. When I invited George into my office for our third conversation, I could see anger in every line of his face.

I didn't have to invite him to speak what was on his mind.

"God damn it, Wes. God damn the whole thing."

This was not profanity. It was a prayer.

"What George? What's happening?"

"The hospice people told us that seizures were a possibility, and they made sure we had all the right medicines to handle it. But it almost sent me over the edge."

"Damn. Almost?"

"You do what you gotta do. The wife and I called the hospice folks, and a nurse was there in twenty minutes. By then the seizure was over, and Shannon was out like a light. When is this going to end?"

"When is the nightmare going to end?"

"Why doesn't God just take her? I've spent months asking God to heal her. And he didn't have the decency to do that. The least he could do is just take her now. My wife would be crushed to hear me say that."

"Crushed?"

"She's still asking Jesus to ride in on his white horse and fix everything. I've about had my fill of Jesus."

"The whole religion thing can seem pretty irrelevant when life is this insane."

"What's the point of believing if God can't show up at a time like this?"

"George, may I ask a really hard question? I want you to keep in mind that our conversations are not like other sorts of conversations. I need to be able to ask hard questions and trust that you'll stick with me."

"Go ahead."

"Do I recall you saying something like it would have been better if Shannon had never been born?"

"The thought has crossed my mind." He begins to cry. "What kind of a father am I?"

"Perhaps an honest one. Can you tell me why it's so hard to acknowledge such a thought?"

"Because it's so damn selfish, that's why." George glares at me like I don't have a brain in my head.

"That's one way to look at it. Do you think Shannon ever wishes she'd never been born?"

"I don't know. She's never said anything like that."

"It's just so strange. We'd give anything to erase the pain for a child, and for ourselves, and yet the only way to avoid such pain is to avoid life altogether. You and I didn't have a choice. Our parents forced this existence on us. But then we just naively inflict the gift on others by bringing the next generation into the world."

"Shit, Wes. Isn't that kinda harsh?"

"I really don't mean to come off as harsh. How else are we supposed to make sense of things? You are walking through hell right now. Other than your daughter having never been born, has there been a way to guarantee that this nightmare would never have occurred?

"There are no guarantees. I know that. No guarantees. Still, I keep thinking about the sermon our pastor preached the Sunday after we got Shannon's diagnosis. He knew what we were going through, and he preached on that verse…something like, 'I will never leave you. I will never forsake you.' And then he threw in 'I know my redeemer lives.'"

"The book of Hebrews, and that second one is from Job. What was it like for you to hear those words then?"

"It was a comfort. It was truly a comfort." I can tell George is recreating that moment in church in his mind. He almost seems comforted all over again.

"But not so much now?"

163

"Not so much now. Because he *has* forsaken Shannon. He hasn't shown up. He hasn't saved her."

"If that's what you believe, I'm not going to try and talk you out of it. But I do want to know…is that what you *really* believe? Is there really no space for seeing God redeeming Shannon, and you, and your wife, in this?"

"You're startin' to piss me off."

"I'm just asking you to not throw the baby out with the bathwater. Just because you've gotten a few twisted ideas about God, it doesn't mean God isn't in the middle of all this. When the Bible says that God was in Christ, redeeming a broken world so that the world could be in relationship to him, it never says that the brokenness isn't going to kick the shit out of us, or the people we love, in the process."

George is quiet. I have the impression he is trying to soak this in. I continue…

"George, the coming weeks are going to just get harder. More than anything, I know you want to be as present to Shannon as you possibly can be. You have every right to your anger, and your regrets. But if I know you at all, you're just going to end up full of shame if you let the anger and regrets get in the way of being present for her."

"OK. I see what you mean." And I believe him. George suddenly looks like a man who knows he has an important job in front of him.

"At some point you may decide to throw your religion into the garbage. For now, I'm just asking you go with the faith you've been raised in. See if you can just say to yourself, "God is redeeming Shannon, and it doesn't have to feel OK for it to be true."

George is weeping.

"George, may I sit next to you and put my arm around your shoulder?"

He nods. I move next to him. He leans into the crook of my arm. I feel his tears fall on my hand.

REFLECTIONS

I (Milton) tear up every time I read this session with George. I know I feel George's sense of loss. But I think what gets me the most is he is so emotionally rudderless. He is literally at the mercy of every emotional current that comes into his mind.

I also cannot help but think about what college advisers say to their students on many occasions: "I am here to support you. But I am not here to clean up the messes you make because you refuse to choose the things academically that I advise you to do." But the irony of God as redeemer in Job's case is that's exactly what seems to be portrayed: Job is having to clean up the mess that God has made of Job's life. And part of that cleanup process for Job may simply be recognizing that his own redemption comes from within himself. If only he had someone to sit beside him and let him cry.

The question of what an individual would give up in order to avoid such pain is poignant. And only retrospectively do individuals confront the question—never prospectively. We don't ask before we become parents about the potential pain that might accompany the enjoyment of our children. And even if we did, we would be discouraged from worrying so. Who can predict the future? But pain may be the price of having evolved to such a state that such enjoyment is even possible, the evolutionary biologists tell us.

24

Finding God

Job 23:3

Oh, that I knew where I might find him, that I might come even to his dwelling!

Connections

Wouldn't it be amazing to live in a world where you could expect every person you encountered to treat you with love, or at least respect? Supposedly this is what the Kingdom of God should be like. For now, we feel fortunate if folks are simply willing to play by the rules. And even this seems more than we can hope for. But surely we can expect more from those who tell us they love us, can't we?

The homily imagines God as an absentee landlord who seldom, if ever, shows up to repair his rental properties. The counseling session asks us to consider what it's like when a spouse is the one who is not keeping a promise.

How are we to react when a trusted person wants to break a promise? And what if the promise-breaker is God? Could it be that we sometimes assume our vision of a promise is the same as the other's vision?

THE HOMILY

When I read this verse, I always wonder what Job really wants for all of his lamenting.

The first house my young family and I ever lived in was a rental. It was an older house, but had ample room and was in a good location near the college where I was starting my new teaching job. A friend secured it for us, as we were just moving back into the country.

I noticed a mix of funny odors when I first walked in—all were unidentifiable. There was metal siding on the outside that seemed out of character with the age of the house. But, at the time, I did not think about what might be beneath it. It was OK, I thought, and the arrangement with the landlord—all the signing had been done through the mail, and his realtor turned the house over to us—was difficult with his living a few hundred miles away in the next state over. I came to hate that house, though, especially when things began to fall apart and neither the landlord nor his agents could be found anywhere. The problems were severe enough that I just wanted out of the lease before things got even worse. Absentee landlords have come to be the bane of tax bases and urban beautification projects. They own property in one location but never live there. The profits they make do not go back into the properties they own but benefit areas far away. They fight tooth and nail to retain the *status quo* of their profitable property ownership. And all of that goes on while their tenants suffer through the discomforts of the owners' abdication of responsibility. Profit without responsibility is the quickest way to make a financial killing, it seems. And that is the well-worked strategy of the absentee landowner.

Job's cry to find God may be like that of a tenant whose house has fallen into serious disrepair and he just wants the property owner to show up and do the job he agreed to do. It's not a request for a special companionship, just one of mutual observance of contractual obligations. Job seems to understand that God has agreed to govern the world with justice; that one's personal health and happiness are directly related to an individual's moral course in life. And Job feels that God has violated his end of the bargain. Job feels his suffering is in violation of the agreement. He has, he asserts, kept his own end of the bargain by living an exemplary virtuous life. And now that things are all broken, he is wondering where God is and why he won't show up and make things right.

So when Job cries out to find God, it's not as though he expects any sympathy from God. He wants to take him to court. There's no sentimentality involved in this case. It's just a matter of what is fair.

Job files a lawsuit against his absentee Lord and talks as though God is hiding somewhere. If only someone would bring him in so he could stand before a judge at court, Job would lay his case before Him, and fill his mouth with arguments (v. 4). There, Job says, *an upright person could reason with him, and I should be acquitted forever by my judge* (v. 7).

The problem is even more complicated, though. It's not just that God is himself an absent landlord, but he is also the judge. And when judges go missing, who has the power to bring them in? And thus Job concludes, *But he stands alone and who can dissuade him? What he desires, that he does* (v. 13).

When we talk of relationship with God, what do we mean? Are we speaking of a rather legal kind of relationship, like the one Job assumes? A relationship where each party has entered into an agreement and is bound by that agreement? That's all that Job wanted, and that was impossible for him to find. I doubt, though, that such a relationship would be particularly satisfying for contemporary persons of religious faith. And yet, people of religious faith do want so much more from God.

WALTER AND CRYSTAL

A contract is a transaction. A covenant is a relationship.

RABBI JONATHAN SACKS

"I know! I know! I made the promise! I'm not saying I didn't make the damn promise!"

Crystal had grown tired of Walter's speech, which I must admit sounded a lot like a prosecutor's opening statements. Her sister was sitting in the waiting room with their four-week-old baby boy, and Crystal kept gazing at the door that was separating her from her precious bundle of joy. However, about the fourth time Walter used the phrase, "she promised," Crystal had suddenly became very present. She continued.

"I love my work! I thought six weeks of maternity leave would have me climbing the walls. I had no idea I would feel like this!"

In Walter's "opening arguments," I learned he and Crystal had decided to start a family last year. They wanted to upgrade from their tiny cottage and had found a wonderful house they both loved. It was a little more expensive than they had anticipated spending, but quite doable on their dual incomes. They moved into the new place, and soon Crystal was pregnant. Evidently Walter was almost goofy in his adoring nurture of Crystal as his first child grew inside her. Neither of them anticipated the wildfire that would be sparked by the blessed birth of a healthy baby boy.

"I would have never agreed to buy the house, at least not *this* house, if I'd known she wouldn't be going back to work. We *need* her income."

"But we *can* do it Walter! I've worked out a budget. We can make it work!"

"Crystal, your budget doesn't make any sense."

I figure it's time for me to say something. "What doesn't make sense about it?"

"She's got us cutting everything back to bare bones. No money going to savings. No eating out. No movies. No vacations. We'd be making minimum payments on our student loans."

"Her plan seems both irresponsible and unfair to you? Crystal, do you think that's a fair assessment?"

"Maybe a little, but shouldn't our child be worth it?"

Walter is so agitated. "Crystal, that's just not fair, and you know it! *You* are the one who used to talk about your 'hero,' Kathy, the working mom with three amazing kids. Don't make this about me not loving our child enough."

"Guys," I interject, "You've done a great job here of helping me understand the dilemma. And you're also helping me see why it's so hard for you to work together on this. You sound more like two people arguing about a broken contract than a couple working through the difficulties of living out a covenant. Crystal, it's obvious you are trying to break a promise, and that should not be taken lightly. But, Walter, you seem more invested in 'upholding the law' than meeting your wife in her pain and confusion. Does it seem to y'all that my perspective fits?"

They are both focused on me, looking puzzled, yet open. I continue.

"There's no question that making and keeping promises is one of the most important aspects of maturity, and business contracts are structured specifically around promises. Contracts, though, don't require people to love each other. Covenants, however, assume that life is far more mysterious than we can imagine, and that even the best intended promises can be sideswiped by unexpected developments. Covenants are about honoring a relationship, not rules. One way I know a covenant is being significantly stressed is when people get overly focused on keeping promises."

"Are you saying I shouldn't care that Crystal wants to break her promise?"

"Not at all. It matters a lot. But here's what I want to know, Walter. Have you generally found Crystal to be someone who has respected your needs and wants, and who has been willing to make sacrifices for you? Over the course of your relationship, has she loved you well?"

"Yes. Yes, she has."

"Can you trust that she would never take breaking a promise lightly, and if she's trying to, she must be horribly undone by these maternal feelings that have blossomed?"

Walter's silent. I see the wheels turning. I turn to Crystal.

"Crystal, it really does sound like you are questioning Walter's love for your son. Is that really how you see him? Has he typically been someone who just wants his way regardless of what it will cost others?"

"No."

"So, am I correct in assuming that most of the evidence is describing two people of integrity who have somehow managed to get well into life together before something seriously challenged their covenant?"

Walter answers, "I suppose that's true."

"Well, that's the impression I have and, quite frankly, I think it speaks highly of both of you that you've done life so well together up to this point."

Crystal asks, "So what do we do?"

"I don't know what you should do. My guess is that you have the ability to make any number of approaches work. Right now I'm concerned that you have two weeks left of maternity leave and you feel so trapped. Crystal, can you get any additional leave so that we have more time to work through this?

"Maybe. My boss loves me, but she has regularly texted me saying that the place is falling apart without me there. But I think she'd be OK with me taking more time if it is what I need. I'm sure it would be without pay, though."

"Walter, can your finances handle four to six more weeks without Crystal's check?"

"Yeah. We can do that. We've got enough in savings to handle that."

"OK, then here's what I'm suggesting. Crystal, I'd like for you to see what you can work out with your boss. Is that a conversation you could have with her today?"

"Sure, I can go by her office this afternoon. Do you think she'd feel manipulated if I took the baby with me?" I'm seeing Crystal's smile for the first time.

"Walter, is this OK with you?"

"Sure. It never occurred to me that she could take some additional time."

"Well, it *is* hard to think creatively when we're under a lot of stress. Can we set up an appointment for next week?"

They both respond with a simultaneous "Sure!"

"Good, let's see what's open on my schedule. In the meantime, I'd like for you to see if you can have a conversation around a rather lofty question: "What do we want our marriage to stand for?"

REFLECTIONS

The session with Walter and Crystal made me (Milton) remember something my father used to tell us: "Be good to people on your way up, because you're going to need them on your way down." I suppose it struck me like my own marriage vows, which included the very traditional "in sickness and in health." As I began to reflect on the language of both the advice and the promise, I realized that they both seem to assume that bad times will not only eventually be there, but you will need a partner to rely upon when you face them.

The conversation between Walter and Crystal introduces the element of unintended consequences due to responses to rather normal changes that come to pass. But if the marriage relationship and the family budget are metaphors for God's governance of the universe, then religious folk probably need to rethink their expectations. In doing so, don't they need to accommodate for change and the unintended consequences of new possibilities for joy?

Forward, Back, Left, and Right

If I go forward, he is not there; or backward, I cannot perceive him; on the left he hides, and I cannot behold him; I turn to the right, but I cannot see him.

Connections

Why, do you suppose, do we persist in our belief that God must behave in ways that make sense to us—especially when our own experience tells us that we can't even expect the people we know best to behave in ways that make sense to us?

The homily reflects upon Job's grappling with God's absence, while continuing to insist that God *must* show up. God has shown up for others. Why not Job? The narrative steps outside of the counseling office to reflect on the ways we might contribute to the confusion others feel about God's presence, and absence, in their lives.

THE HOMILY

Our translations of these verses capture in familiar images the totality of Job's search for God everywhere: he has looked forward, back, to the left, and to the right with no success. It makes us recall the haunting words of the Exilic Isaiah who asserts: *Truly, you are a God who hides himself, O God of Israel, the Savior* (Isaiah 45:15).

The context of that prophetic oracle, the affirmation of God's hiddenness, is a means of justifying his mystifying political reversals for God's people. The hidden God is inscrutable, and when it's in Israel's favor, hiddenness is a powerful confession of hope and confidence. In Job's bitter laments about his own suffering, however, the idea of God's hiddenness is simply a comfortable way of rationalizing injustice. And Job is not the only one to see it that way. The psalmists intone bitter words of lament due to God's absence: *But I, O LORD, cry out to you; in the morning my prayer comes before you. O LORD, why do you cast me off? Why do you hide your face from me?* (Psalm 88:13-14); Or consider Psalm 10:1-2: *Why, O LORD, do you stand far off? Why do you hide yourself in times of trouble? In arrogance the wicked persecute the poor—let them be caught in the schemes they have devised.*

Job clearly understands God's silence as a breach of their relationship, rather than as a point of hope: *Why do you hide your face, and count me as your enemy?* (13:24)

If we read Job's story against those of other biblical characters, we find that seeing God is not apparently so difficult for some. There's Moses, of course (Exodus 33:21-22), who comes about as close to seeing God's face as anyone (take a look at Exodus 24:9, though). And further in the prophetic tradition there is eighth-century Isaiah, whose oracles state baldly: *In the year that King Uzziah died, I saw the LORD sitting on a throne, high and lofty....* (Isaiah 6:1). And then there's the exilic prophet, Ezekiel, whose words seem to be describing his own vision of God: *There was the appearance of the likeness of the glory of the LORD* (Ezekiel 1:28c). Such testimonies in the biblical story leave the impression that seeing God's face is a possibility for all of God's followers. That's especially so if God's alleged hiddenness can be explained as the result of the occasional moral lapse. Moses' song found in Deuteronomy asserts: *You were unmindful of the Rock that bore you; you forgot the God who gave you birth. The LORD saw it, and was jealous....He said: I will hide my face from them....* (Deuteronomy 32:18; also 31:18).

In fact, several biblical voices testify that seeing God is simply a matter of looking at creation:

The heavens are telling the glory of God; and the firmament proclaims his handiwork (Psalm 19:1). The poet of Psalm 8 sees in the heavens nothing other than God's careful design that elevates humans far above the position that their relative status in the universe deserves. And for Christians, it is a view that carries over as a basis for confidence in a morally ordered universe. The apostle Paul writes: *Ever since the creation of the world, his eternal power and divine nature, invisible though they are, have been understood and seen through the things he has made* (Romans 1:20).

So why would God be so available to Moses, the prophets, and the psalmists, but withdrawn from Job? It's impossible to know why, but it may help us understand why Job could imagine being so terrified when God finally does show up: *Therefore am I terrified at his presence; When I consider, I am afraid of him* (23:15).

A God who is capable of such good things, but who can also justify his absence in the face of extreme suffering is a God who makes his people very cautious. The words of Ecclesiastes soberly remind: *Guard your steps when you go to the house of God; to draw near to listen is better than the sacrifice of fools....* (Ecclesiastes 5:1).

THE STRANGER

"Was that the doorbell?"

"What?" Holly is rousing me from a deep slumber.

"The doorbell. The doorbell just rang. Should we check it?"

"We?" I glance at the clock. Two-thirty. I crawl out of bed and stumble into the hallway. I flip on the light and notice an old tennis racket in the corner. Should I carry it with me? I leave the lights off in the living room in order to see better out the window. I recognized the young man immediately.

A couple of evenings earlier, we were having friends for dinner when my wife saw a young man trudging up our front walk with an old lawnmower. Holly met him at the door and immediately noticed the bloody sock on his left ankle. He asked if we needed our lawn mowed. Holly said we did not, but then she pointed at his ankle.

"You OK?"

He shrugged. "I guess."

"I'm a nurse. Would you like for me to look at it?"

I watched from the door as they sat on the front steps and Holly gently removed a battered tennis shoe and slowly slipped off the grimy sock. There was a nasty gash on his ankle.

"May I take a look at your other foot also?"

He shrugged again. Soon Holly was examining both of his feet.

"Sit right here. I've got some medicine inside. If we don't clean this up, then you're going to get an infection." She brushed past me through the front door, and I stepped outside."

"When did that happen?"

"Not sure. Yesterday?" Everything about this rather large man, with a face full of innocence, had the feel of a child.

"It must be painful."

"Not so bad."

Holly came out with a tub of warm soapy water, a washcloth, Neosporin, and bandages. She knelt down and tenderly washed his wound, and then both of his feet. She asked me to get a pair of my socks. When I returned they were sitting quietly as Holly started to wrap the bandages around the wound, shiny from the ointment. I was aware that our friends were chatting quietly in the house.

Holly massaged his feet and slipped the clean sock on. She knocked the dirt out of his shoes and, again, gently, worked his toes back into them.

"Elton, are you hungry?" She must have gotten his name while I was getting the socks.

"Yeah."

"Stay right here." I wasn't sure if that was directed at him or me.

Holly returned with a plate full of food. "You sit right here and eat. We need to get back to our guests. If you want more, just knock on the door." He started digging in. The irony of Holly's comment about getting back to our guests didn't strike me until much later.

Back inside the house, Holly asked, "Do you have a little cash?" I stepped back out on the porch and slipped a twenty next to him. "Here, in case you need gas for your mower." He nodded a thank you with his mouth full. A little later, we and our friends found the empty plate and utensils sitting on the steps.

Wouldn't this be a perfect place for the story to end?

I move cautiously in the dark toward the front door. On the illuminated porch, I can see it's him. Elton, the Stranger, has returned. I'm angry.

I open the door. He offers a sheepish smile. Sternly, I say, "Listen, we were glad to help you out, but you cannot be showing up in the middle of the night. You need to go." I watched him trudge down the sidewalk.

Holly has switched on her bedside lamp. "Everything OK?"

"Oh, it was that guy you helped the other evening."

"Elton? Elton showed up in the middle of the night? What did you tell him?"

"I told him that we were glad to have helped him, but he couldn't just be showing up in the middle of the night."

"That's sorta weird."

Holly switches off the lamp, and we settle under the covers. An unsettling thought crosses my mind, and I speak it in the dark.

"I'm going to be really pissed if it turns out that was Jesus."

The bed begins to shake, just a little at first, and then Holly bursts into laughter, which then turns into the oxygen-starving guffaws that leave tears in our eyes.

"I know…I know," she gasps. "It's awful for me to laugh, but that was just not what I expected to come out of your mouth!"

REFLECTIONS

I've (Wes) continued to be troubled by this encounter over the years. What does it say about me? What does it mean about me that we left Elton on the porch to eat alone? What does it mean that I felt so proud of my wife's care for him, and then so indignant at his return in the middle of the night?

But it wasn't until I read Milton's homily that I wondered what it all meant to him, Elton. I wonder if he was inclined to receive Holly's care as some sort of mysterious expression of the grace of God. If so, what would my terse rejection have been like for him? Undoubtedly, unlike Job, Elton had been far too beaten down by life to demand that God explain his mysterious ways.

26

If I Have Walked with Falsehood

Job 31:5

If I have walked with falsehood, and my foot has hurried to deceit—let me be weighed in a just balance, and let God know my integrity!

Connections

Ever notice how differently things appear to you as you've aged? A four-year-old and a forty-year-old have very different ways of defining *good*. At least we hope they do. A four-year-old thinks a lot like any animal thinks: Good is me getting what I want, no matter what. We have a word for forty-year-olds who think this way—*sociopaths*. By the time people are forty, we hope they have embraced some larger view of *good*. We hope they are able to see morality in terms of what is good for everyone, not just themselves.

The honor code at a college is one way our culture tries to help young people move toward a mature view of morality. We hope such codes help students understand that honesty is the right way to live. However, for many students, the honor code never becomes more than a set of rules for staying out of trouble.

Is it any wonder that we become confused when we see grown-ups treating cultural honor codes as though they reflect obnoxious obstacles? And shouldn't we be angry when individuals or groups are rewarded for finding the most creative ways to trash morality?

Job's words seem academic in view of the many different ways that people can tell the truth without telling the whole truth. Real tragedies seldom turn on the difference between good and evil, but rather on the difference between good and good. What is true, in other words, is often much more difficult to discern than what many persons believe the truth actually is. In the counseling session, the real truth of Gabriel's situation may never be known, but he has to face his life as it comes.

The Homily

The honor code at William Jewell College recognizes only three types of dishonor: lying, cheating, and stealing. The aim of the code is to emphasize students choosing what is morally good. And the good features a kind of integrity students are to embrace. We desire that students freely and independently act with integrity at all times. Honesty forms the grounding principle for academic integrity.

In the same way that Jewell's honor code makes sense if one knows the nature of goodness that is behind it, the poet of Job also assumes his readers understand what that good consists of for Job's context. We begin to get an idea as we read the list of behaviors Job forswears in this his closing defense. It should be no surprise that after Job's opening language of personal covenant (vv. 1-4), he asserts the principle of honesty. For Job, it seems, the grounding notion of good begins with absolute honesty. There is no room for any kind of deceit or dissimulation. Whatever the ultimate good is, for Job, it cannot be reached or maintained apart from honesty.

Honesty begins with himself and his private behavior:

I have made a covenant with my eyes…

JOB 31:1

If my step has turned aside from the way, and my heart has followed my eyes…

JOB 31:7

If I have concealed my transgressions as others do, by hiding my iniquity in my bosom…

JOB 31:33

And that private behavior includes the most serious kinds of idolatries:

If I have made gold my trust…if I have rejoiced because my wealth was great…

JOB 31:24-25

If I have looked at the sun when it shone, or the moon moving in splendor, and my heart has been secretly enticed…

JOB 31:26-27

Job's honesty continues into the area of his very public relationships and responsibilities:

If I have rejected the cause of my male or female slaves, when they brought a complaint against me…

JOB 31:13

If I have withheld anything that the poor desired, or have caused the eyes of the widow to fail...

Job 31:16

I once listened in on a panel discussion between two well-known regional political campaign advisers. They both discussed their roles in the 2008 contest between Missouri incumbent congressman Sam Graves and the democratic challenger, Kay Barnes. Barnes lost that year. Democrats were heartened nevertheless since, despite the loss in Missouri, the national presidential campaign went to the democratic candidate.

Missourians, though, witnessed on the congressional level one of the nastiest political fights we had seen in some time. In the course of the panel discussion about that campaign, the two campaign advisers for the congressional candidates admitted to what I thought were shady dealings. They both insisted upon the admissibility of using half-truths and innuendo in portraying the opposing candidates. Their strategy was merely to create a negative impression of the opposing candidate. When questioned by the audience about the ethics of such behavior, they both agreed that it was up to the voter to discern what was true and false. The whole truth was not their responsibility. They could say practically anything they wanted.

I could not really judge whether the audience was as aghast as I was. But I honestly felt like I had just stepped off the bus into the big city for the first time. I just wanted someone to tell me that this was not really so.

Perhaps I'm overstating a bit, because I have known for some time that politicians traffic in half-truth as a matter of course. I think it's part of their job description. And, for that matter, I have long known that *how* a lawyer presents the facts in a legal argument is the difference between convincing a jury of guilt or innocence. We don't call that lying. We call it providing an effective defense.

And, while we're at it, consider how theologians interpret the ambiguities of the Bible. Interpretations are often, if not usually, shaped by the difference between conservative and progressive approaches to scripture. When theologians emphasize scripture that supports their views, and ignore those that don't, we don't accuse them of lying, do we? Yet who has the time to truly examine all of the assumptions behind the claims?

Teachers in primary and secondary schools cannot tell the whole story about a host of topics, due both to time available and developmental readiness of their students. As a matter of fact, what we choose to reveal and conceal from prospective employers is simply a matter of wise job application, isn't it? Is any of this lying?

How should we decide? We usually decide about such things when what others have chosen to conceal slams in on our lives like a hurricane.

GABRIEL

If having a soul means being able to feel love and loyalty and gratitude, then animals are better off than a lot of humans.

JAMES HERRIOT

"Sometimes it sounds like you are upset things like this happen, and sometimes it sounds like you are mainly upset that it happened to you."

Gabriel has been seething with anger ever since I met him a few weeks ago. His Brazilian accent is strong, but only gets in the way of my understanding his words when emotions are running high. He'd recently been let go from the computer company he'd been with for a little over a year.

"Either way, what difference does it make? There's no sense of loyalty in this country."

Gabriel had gladly taken on the difficult path to citizenship in the US, but right now it's hard to imagine him ever having been proud to achieve it.

"It makes a difference to you. Perhaps especially to you. I've worked with very few people who've left home seeking opportunity in this country. From what I can tell, you've worked hard and played by the rules. And, am I remembering this right that you send a sizable portion of your income back to your family in Brazil?"

"I won't be sending anything back for a while. My parents are upset."

"Upset because they know how hard this is on you?"

"I'm not sure." Gabriel stares at the carpet…

"Not sure about what?"

"I know my mother is mainly worried about me, but she also has to figure out how to buy school clothes for my brothers and sisters. My father, though…"

"What about your father?"

"He keeps asking me what I did wrong." Gabriel mutters something in Portuguese.

"He thinks you brought this on yourself?'

"He won't come out and say it, but I can tell he's thinking it."

I'm distracted for a moment. Ever since I started reading Job again, it seems I'm constantly running into him in my office.

"Just to double-check, do *you* think you did anything wrong that resulted in your termination?"

"Absolutely not. I was at the office early every day, and I often stayed late. My projects never missed deadlines, and they were usually ahead of schedule. I was respectful of my boss and coworkers. Yet that *idiota* Sam still has his job and I don't. They are all bigots. They think everyone with dark skin and an accent snuck across the border illegally."

"Whoa…What was said to you that gave you that impression?"

"Nothing, but what else could it be? My boss wouldn't even talk to me about it. He gave me the standard company line about changes in direction and ended the meeting. When I demanded an explanation, he had me escorted from the building." Gabriel is still not looking me in the eyes.

"You hadn't told me about that." I can see tears forming now. "Here we call that adding insult to injury." Just when I think he is about to weep, a look of defiance returns to those moist eyes.

"*Bastardos.*" It crosses my mind that this is a weird way to learn Portuguese.

"Gabriel, you are at something of a crossroads."

"What do you mean?"

"Well, you've taken a real body blow, and nobody gets to tell you how much pain to feel, or how long you should feel it. Yet you seem focused on questions that have no answer."

"You don't think I deserve justice?"

"It's not about what you deserve or not. It's about how we react to situations over which we have no control. You played by rules, and you lost your job anyway. Your dad keeps suggesting you must have done something wrong. No one is willing to provide you with satisfying explanations. Your small self needs comfort right now, but I'm wondering if you're letting the wounded little guy hijack the bus."

"And so what if I am?"

"You'll end up in a ravine?"

"Who cares?" I'm still waiting for Gabriel to lift his eyes to meet mine.

"I'm pretty sure you do. You may have been truly victimized in this situation, but it's not your style to simply *be* a victim."

"So you are telling me to get over it?" Now his blue eyes drill into mine.

"No, not at all. I'm asking you not to lose sight of who you really are…your *Authentic Self*. It's never a good idea to tell the small self to just shut up and go away, any more than it's healthy for a parent to tell a hurting child to shut up and go away."

"You should meet my father."

"And maybe it would be good for us to talk more about your father. But for now I'm asking you to keep something in mind. The longer we are disconnected from our most authentic goals, the more we let shame infect the situation. I've really come to believe this. The price we pay for living outside of our most authentic values is shame."

REFLECTIONS

Losing a job is almost always a very serious thing. Gabriel's sense of injustice is fueled by his anxiety over the future. How will he survive? The truth is Gabriel will, in all likelihood, do just fine. He is a hard worker and an exceptionally intelligent guy. He might even come to believe this firing was a good thing!

But Gabriel's pain is intensified by the deep sense of injustice he feels, and it is multiplied by his father's quiet accusations. Could we find a closer real-life comparison to the attitude of Job's friends?

Gabriel's language is like the lamenting of the biblical psalms. It is voiced in words that convey deep pain yet also demand explanation. And when we demand explanation, it seems we end up having to choose between two equally unsatisfying conclusions. We either take Gabriel's path, asserting that we've been done wrong, or we take the path of his father, asserting that we must have done this to ourselves.

What if we didn't require an explanation? What if we could focus on the pain and challenge of our current reality? What if we could be curious enough to learn whatever is there for us to learn, and get on about the business of life? The small self demands an explanation. The Authentic Self asks, *How can I best move forward from here?*

27

Arrogance in Religion

Job 32:2

Then Elihu, son of Barachel the Buzite, of the family of Ram, became angry. He was angry with Job because he justified himself rather than God.

Connections

Have you ever found your anger surprising you? Anger can be such a confusing emotion. Some people are so afraid of their anger that they can't acknowledge its presence. Others seem to lead with anger in every painful situation, as if mere bluster will reshape circumstance.

How can we tell when a person's anger is fueled by authentic commitment to an ideal, and when it's more about immaturity and arrogance? Milton's homily expresses curiosity about an angry young

Elihu. The counselor pushes an angry young woman to step back from her anger and ask some fresh questions.

THE HOMILY

After an absolutely riveting minute-and-a-half piano solo, Billy Joel's "Angry Young Man," a hard-driving rock music paradigm, lays out for listeners a picture with which we're all too familiar. The next-to-the-last stanza goes like this:

And there's always a place for the angry young man,
With his fist in the air and his head in the sand.
And he's never been able to learn from mistakes,
So he can't understand why his heart always breaks.
And his honor is pure and his courage as well,
And he's fair and he's true and he's boring as hell,
And he'll go to the grave as an angry old man.[12]

Elihu, Job's fourth friend, evokes much comment for two things, mainly: his anger and his youth. We may find, though, that the most apt appraisal of the fourth friend is accurately captured in the lyric, *he's boring as hell*...We are given no indication of anything other than his relative youth. He speaks last because the other friends were older than him (32:4b). We cannot really determine whether he is young or not. In fact, he does not really say anything that advances the conversation constructively. He certainly does not provide a convincing answer for Job, and that is probably because his views are so much like those of the other three friends. In fact, that he waits for his other friends to speak without interrupting them is one of the best arguments that he is not particularly youthful. Listening to others and reflecting upon their words is, especially these days, a sign of patience and maturity (my middle age is showing, I know).

So, we might ask those who see Elihu as a youthful friend what they are seeing that makes them say this. I think one thing we associate with youthful behavior has not so much to do with *what* one believes as it does with *how* one believes it. *How* religious folk hold their convictions

---

[12] http://www.elyrics.net/read/b/billy-joel-lyrics/angry-young-man-lyrics.html. Viewed 2.27.13.

of faith may be as important as, if not more than *what* those elements of faith actually are. So if the advice of the sages is important in this respect, then there is a kind of caution that stems from the awareness of one's limited perspective. For instance, one proverb observes, *The one who first states a case seems right, until another comes and cross-examines* (Proverbs 18:17). It's an observation that comes from a court setting and displays much experience at listening to arguments. But it evokes so much more. You cannot actually decide the case until you've heard all sides of the argument. And, short of that, one lives in a state of incomplete knowledge, having to suspend one's judgment.

When does one finally adopt such a perspective on matters that pertain to God and God's governance of the universe? If anything, Elihu's words seem arrogant more than youthful. He presumes to offer a final word, as though there could even be such a thing. Perhaps such arrogance is the best argument for Elihu's youthfulness. It seems a profound arrogance leading to presumption that matters of ultimate concern can be finalized in some fashion. (But then, Elihu's older friends are no different on this point, are they?)

Such arrogance is not foreign to Christianity's history. We see it in the thirteenth-century debate in Barcelona, held before King James I of Aragon, between the Franciscans and the Dominicans. It was a theological debate between the Jewish scholar Moses Nachman (remembered in the acronym RaMBaN) and his challenger Friar Paulo Christiani. One of the main questions in the debate was whether the messiah had already come. Apparently, on the fourth day of the disputation, Nachman appealed to biblical evidence and Talmudic commentary. He began to get the better of his Christian rival. So the king suspended the debate, and it was never finished. King James, though, awarded Nachman three hundred dinars for the way he debated. The bishop of Gerona requested Nachman to write his views in a book, which he did. Two years later, the Dominicans brought him to trial for writing these views, which, they said, were evidence of abuses against Christianity. Nachman argued that his words were spoken because the king had promised him freedom of speech and that he only wrote his words at the request of the bishop. Only then was the king able to extricate Nachman from the trial. But the Dominicans did not give up. They appealed to Pope Clement IV on the matter, and the pope wrote a letter to King James requesting that

Nachman be punished for writing the words against Jesus. Nachman fled to Israel, where he remained the rest of his life.

Has Christian religious faith behaved more like an angry young man, believing opinions about God to be finite, than a patient friend and member of the family of faiths?

BETH

I see myself capable of arrogance and brutality. ...That's a fierce thing, to discover within yourself that which you despise the most in others.

GEORGE STEVENS

"Speaking of fairness, Beth, why do you continue to snap at me when I'm trying to be as honest with you as I can be?"

"Because I want an answer."

"I disagree. You don't want an answer. You want an answer that you like."

For those who believe that counseling is supposed to make people feel better, I'd wish for them a chance to observe my conversations with Beth. She's an angry economics professor who is convinced Jesus was a Marxist, and was directed to get counseling after she declared that no Christian would ever accept a salary like that of her school's new president. I'm sympathetic to her anger over how Christian institutions handle financial decisions, but I'm also reminded of how a friend once counseled me, "Wes, it's one thing to be provocative in class. It's another thing to commit professional suicide."

"I'm just sick of you telling me to suck it up and get over it."

"See, that's what I mean. I've never once told you to 'suck it up,' and you've never heard me say 'get over it.' You decide. Are you willing to hear me, or are you going to keep lumping me in with everyone else who doesn't know what to do with your anger?"

The above is an exchange from my second session with Beth. I'm looking forward to today's visit. She'd shot me an email last Thursday telling me she'd been called on the carpet and was meeting with the president on Friday.

"So, you had the meeting with the president, and he didn't provide you with any answers?"

"OK, so maybe he didn't provide me with any answers that I liked. What an arrogant jerk."

"A jerk?"

"He started by blowing smoke. He told me that he'd read a couple of the articles I'd published, and that he'd talked to my dean. He said that as far as he could tell, I was a brilliant thinker, and he knew my student evaluations were strong."

"You're right. He sounds like a major loser. How else did he try to intimidate you?"

Beth glares at me. "He asked me if I had anything I wanted to say to him."

"Oh, gawd."

"Shut up. I asked him if he thought Jesus was happy about the president of a so-called Christian university being paid thousands and thousands of dollars when people in the neighborhood around the school were living in poverty."

"Did he explode?" I'm sure my eyebrows are arched to the ceiling.

"Not really."

"Not really?"

"He said he asked himself that question all the time. He told me he'd never imagined he'd be earning a salary like this, but that at each stage of his career, when he'd experienced success, the money came with it. He told me that what he was really interested in was the influence. Each step along the way, he was gaining access to more and more decision-makers. He began to see how he could help shape policies that affected thousands of people. He also admitted that keeping it all in perspective was a challenge."

"Wow."

"And he added that, even though it was none of my business, he and his wife felt very good about the portion of their income they gave away."

"Did he threaten to fire you?"

"No. He said that life is short, and it doesn't make sense for anyone to remain at a place she can't respect. He said he would regret me leaving, but he also told me if I honestly can't find my way toward some peace here, and some respect for him, then he hoped I would make the decision to leave on my own."

"Not what you expected?"

"Nope. I guess he wasn't what I expected."

"But you don't trust him."

"Hell no I don't trust him!"

"Let me get this straight. This guy, who probably has better things to do than address the complaints of an arrogant, young economics prof, takes time out of his schedule to spend time with you, and all you can do is assume the worst of him? There's no room for you to imagine a man who is trying to listen to God unless he comes to the same conclusions as you?"

"Jesus told the rich man to give away all of his possessions."

"Beth, when are you going to talk about what's really going on with your anger? You're a smart woman. You know that you are unfathomably rich compared to the rest of the world. You haven't given away all of *your* possessions. It just doesn't make sense to me that you are so hung up on how someone else is managing his wealth. What am I missing here?"

"Why do counselors always think that everything is about something else?"

"Well, because many times it's true." I'm leaning in as far as I can without falling out of my cheap recliner. "Beth, when someone is as angry as you are, I always start by assuming the anger is an appropriate response to the situation. However, in many cases, things start getting fuzzy for me. I have come to learn that, for some people, anger is the only emotion they know how to do. Sometimes anger is a cover for fear or sadness—often both. I'm not saying this is the case with you, but I'm sure starting to wonder."

REFLECTIONS

Milton: All right, Wes. This exchange with Beth is confusing me. I've never heard of counselors actually *telling* their clients what to think. You don't portray the artful work of leading her to discover her anger. Your counselor just tells her. What's that about?

Wes: It's always a risky gambit when I decide to take such an assertive stance with a client. However, in this narrative I'm channeling a number of people I've worked with. Individuals who let me know, in one way or another, they considered gentleness a weakness. Beth is a person I've assumed, rightly or wrongly, will get nowhere if the counselor doesn't match her energy, comment for comment. There are some people who don't feel loved unless they are being confronted.

Milton: Yes, but what prevents the counselor from acting out of the same kind of arrogance in such matters as, say, the church did in the case of Nachman above?

Wes: I admitted that it's a risky move. Look, here's what a counselor has to weigh off. The four core emotions are anger, sadness, happiness, and fear (mad, sad, glad, afraid). Three of these are afflictive, meaning they are painful to experience. I believe that we all have our go-to favorite afflictive emotion. For instance, Beth's knee-jerk response to her anxiety is anger.

Milton: So, can we in retrospect assume that church leaders of antiquity, who persecuted others for their non-Christian convictions, were dealing with their own anxiety when they chose some sort of aggressive response, like anger, as a *means* of dealing with it?

Wes: Well, it's a simplistic assessment of history, but I would certainly wonder how much fear and sadness are in the mix. It's quite another thing to consider the interplay of these emotions in the present tense of a client's life. Especially if such emotional complexities are being ignored by someone like Beth. Part of emotional maturity is getting to know ourselves well enough to separate out mad, sad, and afraid and express them to ourselves, others, and God honestly.

28

THE CARNIVAL OF ANIMALS

JOB 39:1

Do you know when the mountain goats give birth? Do you observe the calving of the deer?

CONNECTIONS

Has your minister ever used animals as grounding for his or her formation of theological ideas? The homily tries to consider how their beauty might be more helpful in appreciating God's answer than the concept of justice. From the latter perspective, the animals seem irrelevant; from the former perspective, we have something more to think about.

In the counseling session, Ray is invited to reflect upon the differences in these two approaches to his own bewilderment. It is an interesting teacher who calls this to Ray's attention.

THE HOMILY

It took me a long time to realize that I was reading this section of God's response with music playing in my head. When I would get to the animals, Saint-Saëns's *Carnival of the Animals* would simply start playing. I have heard this musical work in many forms since I was a young child. I am very certain, now, that it has quietly shaped the way I have read this part of the book of Job. For instance, I have too often failed to consider how Job's earliest audiences might have thought of animals. Instead, I could only hear the sounds of the two pianos, strings, clarinet, piccolo, flute, and other orchestral members. The instruments try to imitate modern-day stereotypes of these creatures. And such stereotyping admittedly created a bias in my understanding of the poet's aim in including the animals. And this could explain why my undergraduate Job students always disagree with my reading of this section of the God speeches. They can only hear a continuance of the same, droning, rhetorical questioning from the beginning of God's speeches (38:1-38). They never hear the music that eventually comes into the background.

Consider Job 38:39-40:
Can you hunt the prey for the lion,
Or satisfy the appetite of the young lions,
When they crouch in their dens,
Or lie in wait in their covert?

When I read these lines, instead of focusing upon how God might be using this beast as an argument, I could only hear Saint-Saëns's first movement and the two pianos playing in tandem. The low strings play chords that evoke nobility and triumph.

And when I would read about the wild ass I could only hear the frenetic arpeggios and scales of the two pianos. Or how about Job 39:5-8:
Who has let the wild ass go free?
Who has loosed the bonds of the swift ass,

To which I have given the steppe for its home,
The salt land for its dwelling-place?
It scorns the tumult of the city,
It does not hear the shouts of the driver.
It ranges the mountains as its pasture,
And it searches after every green thing.

The pianos combine to create the impression of velocity and speed out on the open plain. I immediately thought of the pianistic virtuosity required for such performance and transferred this to the beasts themselves. And in my misreading, I heard the same thing when I thought of the ostrich (vv. 13-18) and the horse (vv. 19-25), both of which were animals of speed.

Unfortunately, when I got to the most famous of Saint-Saëns's portrayals of animals, The Swan (*Le Cigne*), I would just forget about Job altogether and lose myself in the music. That was because the peaceful melody played by the cello soloist simply did not match the poem's depiction of any of the other flying animals. The raven (38:41) and the hawk (39:26-30) are birds of prey and are apparently depicted for their own strength and wildness, rather than for their beauty, as the swan.

What a wonderful misreading of God's display of animals I had created! Sure, I overlooked the rhetorical questioning that accompanied them (as my students like to remind me). I therefore tended to read the animals as a meaningful response rather than as a rhetorical device intended to put Job in his place. Thanks to the music, my posture toward the animals was more like that of a patron of an art museum. I was always more interested in peering into the strange beauty of the artwork, trying to discern what the artist saw. It was an experience of otherness and foreignness rather than one of intellectual perplexity and legal maneuvering.

I would find in the animals (appropriately accompanied to the strains of Saint-Saëns) an experience of wonder and awe, of the creator's own delight in his creation. It was probably more like that of the musical composer himself than it was the poet of Job. Somehow in this pastiche of color and sound, the problem of justice was a drab grey. It was there, but suddenly it was much smaller and more difficult to focus upon. I know that God is putting Job in his place by appealing to the animals in this poem. But isn't it possible that an appeal to beauty rather than power is in the mind of the poet?

RAY

When the power of love overcomes the love of power, the world will know peace.

JIMI HENDRIX

"Tell me about someone in your life who had power over you but was also very tender and gentle."

"What do you mean?"

"Well, you've helped me see how your dad never let you forget that he was in charge. How he dared you to take him on so he could put you in your place."

"That's what he did to everyone in the family, especially to mom. Mom just seemed like the oldest child in the room while I was growing up."

"That's the impression I've gotten."

Ray is the oldest child in a family of five siblings. He's been moderately successful in various sales positions, but came to see me when his current boss at a large used car business got in his face. Ray had led the team in sales for a few months last year, but had started showing up late for work while his sales had fallen off. He has responded well to an anti-depressant and a good old cognitive-behavioral approach. But just when I thought he was ready to wrap things up with me, he told me he wanted to talk about dad. Turned out he had plenty to talk about.

"I can still hear him daring her to take a swing at him, just like he dared me and my brothers."

"But was there anyone in the picture who used his authority in a positive way? I'll never forget Mr. Livingston,[13] my high school

---

[13] Mr. Livingston is the real name of my real, high school chemistry and physics teacher. I have no idea where he is now, and whether or not he is even alive. It is an honor to mention him in this story.

chemistry teacher. He was a bear of a man who'd made a ton of money as a government researcher, and then retired to teach school just because he loved kids. I'd made a C on his first test. He called me out into the hall and said, 'Eades, I've looked at your file, and I've seen your IQ score. From this point forward, this is a pass-fail class for you. You will either make an A for me or you will make an F.' He wasn't angry. He wasn't intimidating. He was almost loving! Mr. Livingston was letting me know that he was quite willing to use his authority to motivate me. I made straight As for him in both chemistry and physics. I'll never forget him."

"OK, I'm thinking of someone. When I was playing football in high school, we had this really high-strung coach, Coach Blackmon, who was always screaming and threatening to make us run steps. He made me so nervous that I was always screwing up. My junior year this young guy, Coach Sams, joined the staff. He'd been a star receiver in college, and even played a year in the pros before he blew out his knee. It was a whole different kind of intimidation being on the field with a guy I'd watched on TV." Ray is getting very animated! "The first practice that year, I dropped a pass and Blackmon yelled something like, "You gonna spend another year as a screw-up?" Coach Sams pulled me aside at the end of that practice and said something like, 'You've got skills, kid. But you're playing like you're scared. I've been there, and you and me are going to get you past it.' He laughed and said, 'Or maybe you'd rather just run steps!' Blackmon was just a blowhard, but Coach Sams…he was…he was…"

"An artist?"

"Yeah, an artist. Sometimes, when I was out of sorts, he'd remind me who he was and where he'd been, but it wasn't to intimidate me. He just wanted me to know I could trust him."

"Thank God for the Mr. Livingstons and the Coach Sams in the world."

"I haven't thought about Coach Sams in a long time."

"I wonder if this has anything to do with your disinterest in church these days."

"What do you mean?"

"Well, if every time God is mentioned you conjure up this subconscious image of your Dad, I would think it would be smart to stay away! But what if God is more like Coach Sams?"

Ray laughs. "I suppose I'd be glad to run steps for a God like that!"

"My point exactly."

REFLECTIONS

When I first read Wes's narrative, I (Milton) was troubled by his advice, which evokes thoughts of "a picture is worth a thousand words." At first reading, this seemed shallow: "Just change your picture of God, and you'll feel better!" And yet, I know that the right image, the correct picture, seems to allow the right words to follow. That Wes seems to be taking this as a therapeutic approach is provocative to me.

When I (Wes) first read Milton's homily, I was puzzled. In his admitted misreading by hearing attractive music, Milton was seeing a God who is trying to lure Job close with beauty rather than intimidate him through brute force. Although the brute-force picture may indeed be the most accurate, how does it fit with the Jesus we find in the Gospels?

Jesus' most caustic words are remembered as targeting those arrogantly religious folks who not only believe they actually understand God, but also feel justified in imposing their views on others. With those who know they are sinners, Jesus lures them close with gentle grace.

29.

The Ostrich's Wings Flap Wildly

Job 39:17

...because God has made it forget wisdom, and given it no share in understanding.

Connections

Do you ever overhear persons of religious faith speak of mystery within their faith? One of the gifts religious faith gives to people is a sense of mystery and wonder. We may imagine that Job himself experiences this, perhaps, when he ponders what possible significance the ostrich could have to do with his many questions about God's justice.

In the counseling session, Sharon's immediate adoption of strategies to ease to her grief does more than merely indicate how deeply she feels her pain. It is evidence of how attached she is to some expectations about how the world must be and yet is not.

THE HOMILY

When I get to God's remarks about the ostrich as part of the answer to Job's queries, I smile. I suddenly feel like I'm in the middle of Douglas Adams's *The Hitchhiker's Guide to the Galaxy* (1979). In that story we read about Arthur Dent's journey to Magrathea and Startibartfast's story of the beings there. Deep Thought, their supercomputer, is provocative, to say the least. That's the computer designed to calculate the "ultimate answer to the ultimate question about life and everything." Its calculation of the answer to everything makes me feel as I imagine Job must feel when God says: ...*because God has made it [the ostrich] forget wisdom, and given it no share in understanding* (39: 17).

This seems almost as random as Deep Thought's assertion that the ultimate answer to the universe is the number 42. What on earth could such a number possibly mean? By the same token, how is the ostrich an answer to the problem of injustice and suffering? Does the ostrich give us any insight into the question of fearing God for nothing?

We have at least two options, though. The first is to place God's response, like that of supercomputer Deep Thought, in the realm of mystery. By proposing an answer that seems so silly in its simplicity, the poet conveys ironically the human inability to grasp the complexities of God's governance. Job's questions lose their meaning in relationship to the mystery that must lie at the heart of such an answer. Job's failure to comprehend the significance of the answer could be another way to signify his own ultimate moral weakness. Mystery becomes a cipher for human insignificance in relation to the universe. One side of this cipher is it becomes a religious excuse to avoid reasoning in matters of religious faith. The other side, though, is that mystery allows humans to let go of their resistance to accepting things as they are. That leads to a second option.

I call the second option the WYSIWYG option (what you see is what you get). The answer is really as simple as it appears on the surface. The ostrich, which God seems to be as concerned about as he is Job, has nothing to do with the just governance of the universe. The principles by which Job thinks the universe is governed simply cannot apply. How could a human category like justice apply to the ostrich, from which God has withheld wisdom? Part of the problem, then, is the high expectations Job has based upon his notion that justice prevails in the universe. The ostrich indicates that such a notion simply cannot apply in ways Job thinks it should.

So then we ask, *What about the notion of covenant with God?* Well, yes, there can be covenant, just not a covenant that is based upon a principle of justice. There is no reciprocal rule that enters into a people's relationship with God. So if we continue to have the notion of covenant, what kind of a covenant is it? There has to be some kind of predictability, doesn't there? Doesn't there have to be some rational basis for understanding God? And the answer might be, not necessarily; not if God is free.

Yes, but you might well be saying that this destroys religion, because religion is grounded upon humans' ability to understand God. If God is not understandable, then what kind of relationship can there be? It's no relationship whatsoever, I think. It is the answer "42," and one spends one's life wondering how it could be of any significance. It is a kind of order that appears to be simultaneously random. It is relationship that is open to all kinds of possibilities. None is necessarily predictable, but there is openness to various hypotheses. Life committed to God may be lived out as a test of each one. The answer is the ostrich; she has no *human* wisdom, and God puts her forward as an example of how things really work.

SHARON

And for the tender love that our good Lord hath to all that shall be saved, He comforteth readily and sweetly, signifying thus: It is sooth that sin is cause of all this pain; but all shall be well, and all shall be well, and all manner [of] thing shall be well.

JULIAN OF NORWICH

205

"I suppose that's why so many people raised as Christians are turning to Buddhism, either by a rejection of Christianity altogether, or by adding it in for seasoning," I tell Sharon when I see her, I'm responding to Sharon's thoughtful questions about God.

Sharon is asking the *Why wasn't God paying attention?* question. Her adult son, Stan, had recently gotten a stage IV cancer diagnosis. Sharon is now confronted with a painful experience of disorder in her universe. Parents are not supposed to outlive their children. Her fear and sadness are compounded by anger. It appears that three years ago her son's doctor missed some irregularities in his blood work that would have caught the problem in time for treatment. On this particular day, it seems, Sharon needs to ask some hard questions of God.

"I don't know anything about Buddhism," Sharon whispers.

"There's not all that much in Buddhist thought that is inconsistent with Christianity, but Buddhism starts with radically different ideas about God. At least they are radically different from the brand of Christianity you and I were raised with." My "inner teacher" is stepping to the fore. "For instance, a good Buddhist would never ask why God isn't paying attention. For Buddhists, God simply isn't a person in the way we think of God. We think of God as someone with whom you can have a personal relationship. Buddhists don't. Buddhists tend to think of God as a powerful river, full of life and energy, but not conscious of you or me."

"What's your point?" Sharon seems genuinely curious.

"Well, I feel your anger. And I'm hearing you direct your anger at God. It makes sense to me, but it's terribly unsatisfying, isn't it? I mean, if your husband lets you down, and you express your anger at him, there's at least a chance for some sort of conversation…a chance to understand, and perhaps to work things out."

"You don't know my husband. He's Mr. Ignore and Avoid."

"Now, there's a twist. I can see how it might complicate your spirituality if God seems to embody the most annoying characteristics of your husband. Hmmmmm…"

"Hmmmm…what?"

"Sorry. Before you made that comment about your sweet hubby I was thinking about how we Christians promote the idea of a loving God who is thinking about us, and working on our behalf, and perhaps even slowing our cars down so that we aren't in the intersection when the idiot runs the red light. It's a comfort when things are going well, but when things fall apart…"

"We're angry and confused, with no one to take it out on…"

"Yeah. " I tap my nose to indicate that she's gotten my point. Sharon shifts her gaze out the window. "One time, when Stan was about fourteen, the water park closed two hours before we thought it was going to. When I finally arrived to pick him up, he was sitting on curb, just fuming. He opened the car door and proceeded to, what do kids say? Rip me a new one? I don't even know what that means."

"There's nothing quite like an angry fourteen-year-old."

"I asked him what he thought I was supposed to do. This was way before cell phones. I was out running errands. Even if he'd walked to a convenience store and called home, it wouldn't have done any good."

"Does that sort of fit how you see God right now?"

"I suppose so. But isn't it God's job to stay on top of stuff?"

"Evidently God doesn't think so, or hurricanes wouldn't slam into populated areas. But, Sharon, the more pressing point is that you *are* angry, and sad, and scared."

"Are you saying I shouldn't be?"

"Of course not. I've never found it helpful to judge my feelings or tell myself not to have them. But I also know how twisted up our feelings can get when we are challenged from several directions at once…as we usually are. Stan was angry, and probably afraid, at the water park. His feelings were real; yet directing them at you really missed the point. Right now you are grieving your son's situation, both what you see him living through right now, and what you know is coming. At the same time, you are trying to figure where God is in the mess."

"It *is* a twisted mess."

"What would it be like for you to trust that all will be well, regardless of how the mess plays out?"

"Don't worry, be happy?"

"Hardly. Authentic spirituality doesn't pretend pain doesn't exist. Authentic spirituality helps us sit with our pain and continue to engage life fully. Your son is a strong man, married to a strong woman, but he's still going to need his mother. And his mother is already grieving what she knows is coming. Can we help you be both honest with your grief and fully present for him?"

"I'd like to be able to do that."

"I've just had a thought…Are you familiar with Julian of Norwich?" Sharon looks puzzled. "It looks like Nor-witch, but it's pronounced Nor-itch. Anyway, she was a Catholic mystic living at the time of the Black Plague in Europe. There's even some speculation that she was quarantined in the convent. She's best known for her simple declaration, *'All shall be well, and all shall be well, and all manner of thing shall be well.'* I find myself wondering what you would make of her reflections on God and life."

"I'll look at it. Is there a book I can buy?"

"Her writings are all over the Internet. I'd recommend you read the article on Wikipedia and go from there.

"OK. I'll do it."

"Do you suppose you might be able to take a look before our next meeting?"

"You can count on it."

REFLECTIONS

Once again, I (Wes) am reminded that we don't even know what small theology we carry until a crisis hits, and we certainly don't see how our theology can subtly lead us away from our values. I've sat with more people than I can count who have been filled with shame when they've realized, after the fact, that their anger with God pushed them away from a loved one in need. I see Sharon at risk for such an experience. Her son needs her now as much as he ever has; yet her anger makes it difficult for her to engage with him.

One of the great lessons in my training in hospital chaplaincy was the distinction between anticipatory grief and bereavement grief. Anticipatory grief is the pain we begin to experience when we see the end coming for someone we love. Bereavement grief begins at the point of death, and involves detaching from the physical presence of the person. The great danger is that we will become overwhelmed by anticipatory grief, and begin to slip into bereavement grief before the loved one has died. In such cases, the caregiver begins to emotionally, if not physically, detach too soon. In the aftermath, such a person can feel deep shame and guilt at having abandoned the one he or she loves. One job of the chaplain is to help families cope with anticipatory grief and hang in there.

I see one of my jobs as a therapist as helping people sit with their pain while still holding fast to their deepest values.

30

AND THE LORD RESTORED THE FORTUNES OF JOB

JOB 42:10

And the LORD restored the fortunes of Job when he had prayed for his friends.

CONNECTIONS

Are you troubled by the last chapter of Job's story? Are you among the myriad of people who've thought, *So Job gets a replacement family, and that's supposed to make the obliteration of the first one OK?*

Milton's homily juxtaposes Job's outcome with that of Shakespeare's *Timon of Athens.* In the first, Job gets it all back; in the second, Timon does not.

Wes's narrative taps into the soul of a man who knows his story will not have a happy ending in any conventional sense, but is moving toward peace anyway.

THE HOMILY

A new colleague recently introduced me to a Shakespeare play I had never read. In fact, though I recall having encountered the title in other contexts, she was the first person ever to have referred to the play at all. *Timon of Athens* is about a wealthy citizen of Athens who loses everything because of his generosity and goodness. He is constantly helping his friends out. He underwrites the expenses of artists and hosts dinner parties for his community. His faithful servant, Flavius, tries to warn him of the excessiveness of his generosity, but Timon cannot hear him. And then, it's too late. He is mortgaged to the limit, is in debt, and hasn't a penny to live on.

When he seeks credit from his friends, he is refused. And so, before leaving the city in anger and disappointment at his false friends, he invites them to a feast of warm water and stones, at which he mocks their false generosity. He says:

You great benefactors, sprinkle your society with thankfulness. For your own gifts, make yourselves praised: but reserve still to give, lest your deities be despised

ACT III, SCENE VI

Timon has given his all to others (perhaps unwisely?), yet leaves the city impoverished.

By contrast, Job, who also has lost all, has everything restored by God in the story's ending. This poses for us one of the most perplexing aspects of the story. Why does God restore the fortunes of Job, especially after Job throws the worst of accusations at the heavens? It is not clear. One can only speculate.

It is difficult to find some definitive sense in which God's speech actually agrees with what Job has said. Even God's rhetoric challenges Job and creates the appearance of a stern censure. In fact, the strangest twist of all is that God is actually angry with Job's friends. He says to Eliphaz the Temanite: *My wrath is kindled against you and against your two friends; for you have not spoken of me what is right, as my servant Job has* (JOB 42:8).

Job is then commanded to intercede for his friends. God says he will accept Job's prayer *not to deal with [them] according to [their] folly.*

One way of reading the ending that crops up now and then is that the restoration is an example that God loves *Job* for nothing. The text of the final chapter of the book does not use the word *hinnam* as the prologue does in reference to Job's *fear of God* (1:9). Yet, the implication is clear. There is no good reason for God to have restored Job's wealth. But that God does it anyway is an example of God's disinterested devotion to Job. That is, God does not need a reason to be good to Job in an analogous way that Job does not need a reason, at least not initially, to be devoted to God. Christians refer to this as grace, but one does not really need to find it only in the Christian New Testament. God's grace permeates the stories of the Hebrew scriptures as well.

From a Christian viewpoint, the parallels between Job and Jesus are striking. Both are called servants of God, Jesus at his baptism and Job at the beginning and ending of the story. Both are righteous and suffer unjustly at the hands of God. Both have friends who try to understand their experiences of suffering. Both try to convince God to relent, Jesus in the garden, and Job through his protests and oaths. And perhaps both have some kind of further parallel in that the resurrection functions as a kind of poetic justice for Jesus in the same way that restoration functions as a poetic justice for Job. But what does it mean to say that resurrection provides poetic justice for Jesus? How does such a reading provide meaning for us?

I think I prefer the ending of Shakespeare's play, as Timon is left with several options for how to respond to his fate. Apemantus, the philosopher friend of Timon, counsels contentment in renunciation of desire. Alcibiades, who was banished from Athens, offers Timon military revenge upon the city. Timon rejects both of these responses. Only Flavius, his loyal servant, who sticks by his side uncompromisingly, seems to offer some possible meaning. Flavius offers Timon friendship and loyalty, expecting nothing in return, as Timon honestly faces the reality of humanity's greed. This may not be an ending that settles all questions, to be sure. But it does not leave us with the unreal sense that things always work out for the best. What it does do is place the importance of one's acceptance of his situation and the choice of a response squarely upon one's own shoulders. Perhaps it means that Job himself must create justice in his society, rather than expecting it to be done by God.

RANDALL

People living deeply have no fear of death.

ANAÏS NIN

"But Job got everything back."

"I know. That's one reason I'm not all that comfortable talking about Job with someone in your situation."

Randall could certainly identify with the man sitting on a trash heap after having lost everything; only his story was not going to end like Job's. This rugged man who'd run a half-dozen marathons looked like the picture of health, but the symptoms of Alzheimer's were becoming more pronounced. He knew that if he lived past sixty-five, he'd exist in a fog, surrounded by strangers who call themselves sons and daughters. Those same sons and daughters had badgered him into finally seeing a neurologist when it became clear that more was going on than just the grief of having lost his dear wife to cancer.

"Mary and I had just finished adding the deck to the back of our little house when her diagnosis came back. We'd laughed about how that deck tripled the living space. We'd picked out two rocking chairs, and dreamed about all the kids and grandkids sitting around us this summer." Randall is smiling.

"You know, you don't come off as angry as some might expect you to be."

"What would be the point? What's the point of anything?"

"Good question. Has it ever seemed to you like there was a point?"

"Sure. Even when my business tanked, and we lost the dream home, I remember thinking, 'We've got each other and four kids who are successful professionals. Life is still good.' I'd listen to people at church bitch and moan about their problems. I wanted to say, 'How about you just grow a pair and live the blessed life God is providing.'"

"I'd have paid you a hundred bucks to hear you say that out loud to someone."

Randall laughs. "Yeah, I wish I had too, now. Seems I don't care as much as I used to about what other people might think of me."

"But it does sound like you decided somewhere along the way that God doesn't owe you anything."

"I thought so too, but these days I'm feeling pretty screwed by the Cosmic Big Guy. Look, I'm not all that educated, but I've always been able to see how folks twist the Bible to hear what they want to hear."

"You decided that wasn't exactly the right way to read the Bible?"

"Well, yeah. You can't just go digging around looking for stuff that makes you feel better and ignoring all the stuff that doesn't."

"In my opinion, that's a rather wise way to look at things, but I get the impression that not everyone you go to church with thinks that way. How do you suppose you figured it out?"

"I'm not sure. I've got this magnet on my fridge. My daughter gave it to me right after me and Mary moved into our little place a few years back. It's by some guy named Rohr, and it says, *Faith does not need to push the river because faith is able to trust that there is a river. The river is flowing. We are in it.*"

"You've got a quote by Richard Rohr on your refrigerator?"

"Yeah. A friend of mine saw it and asked me if I was going all Buddhist or something. I still don't know what that means."

"That quote speaks to you."

"It does. Coming back from the hard times, I was seeing how so many people see life like it's this giant game of checkers with God. I remember thinking that if it is, I've lost. When I first read that quote I thought, 'That sure makes a lot of sense.'"

"How so?"

"God is either taking this mess somewhere good, or he's not. I didn't ask to be in this river, but I am. I can trust where it's all going, or I can worry myself sicker than I already am."

"Good point, but you're the one who brought up Job, and that pesky last chapter."

"Pesky…that's a good word for it. It does bother me. Like the poor slob is supposed to be fine with losing his first family by getting a replacement."

"It's troubling, to say the least."

"Do you suppose that last chapter is about heaven?"

"What do you mean?"

"Well, anyone with half a brain can see that good lives end in tragedy all the time. And I'm not one of those people who say there must have been some horrible sin that we didn't know about. That's just stupid. So maybe whoever wrote that Job stuff is trying to tell us that the whole story, not just our individual stories, is going to be OK."

"You're reminding me of the last scene in that movie, *Places in the Heart*."

"Oh yeah…Where all those people who've been fighting are in church together, sharing the Lord's Supper?"

"That's the one. Listen, Randall, no one really knows what the guy writing Job was thinking. All I know is that your take on it sounds like deep wisdom to me."

"Deep wisdom? Then why can't I sleep? And why do the shakes come over me from time to time." For the first time in this conversation, Randall looks troubled.

"Probably because more is happening right now than your brain can process. I'm pretty sure it's not because you are crazy, or a lousy Christian."

"So what do I do?"

"There's nothing wrong with taking a little medicine to help you sleep, and to calm down those shakes. And it probably won't hurt for you to be talking to someone you trust, and who doesn't have a dog in the fight."

"Like you?"

"I'd be honored to spend time with you like this, but it was your kids who kicked you through my door. What do *you* want to do?"

"You won't say idiot things like Job's friends said to him, will you?"

"I can't promise that I won't be an idiot, but I can usually hold it in check."

"You got any openings next week?"

"I think so. Let me look."

.

REFLECTIONS

Milton: Wes, you sure have brought up Buddhism a lot in this book. Are you concerned our readers will wonder if you are really Christian?

Wes: I think I give people plenty of reasons to wonder if I'm Christian, but I hope my reflections on Buddhism aren't a part of that. Just like Randall, I'm trying to find a way to be honest about my faith. Like so many of my clients, Randall has dipped his toe into a bigger theological question than he knows, and he is not finding meaning in the conventional answers. He is moving toward a view that is indeed characteristic of Buddhism.

Milton: As I understand Buddhist thought, it is vast and very diverse. But I think that Buddhism is not that concerned about God. I mean, whether there is or isn't a God is simply not an issue. Other things are more important.

Wes: Most Buddhist theology is OK with the notion of some fundamental Ground of Being, but Buddhists reject the Christian notion that the Ground of Being is an entity with whom we can have a personal relationship. Most Buddhists would say that we can connect with God in the same way we can connect with a river by simply jumping in. But they would also say, in ways reminiscent of Freud, that if we think the river is personally concerned with us, then we're just projecting our own fantasies and wishes onto creation.

Milton: So Buddhist thought would affirm the notion of disinterested faith; that is, faith that commits without regard for the outcomes. It's just not an issue in the same way that it is for Jews and Christians.

Wes: So it would seem. We Christians like to remember Jesus saying, *God has numbered the hairs on your head*. It's a comfort to think that the Author of all creation is that aware of each one of us. Maybe God truly is that aware of me, but if I then conclude that this must mean God will intervene for me, then I've set myself up for additional suffering.

Milton: I think I get what you mean. But isn't it natural to assume that if God truly loves me, then God will do everything possible to take care of me?

Wes: I suppose, but that doesn't mean this is how God sees things. I think about how a good military leader can care intensely for each of the soldiers, and yet still give an order that will sacrifice them in the name of a larger goal. Could it be that God does indeed care for us personally, and yet accepts that the redemptive movement toward the Kingdom will necessarily create pain and suffering for all, and rarely in ways that seem fair?

Milton: Couldn't we do something more with the metaphors we use, though? Why illustrate the paradox of personal versus impersonal with such an institutional model of conflict? Why not a metaphor that is more organic, like, say, evolution? Suffering is how humans understand the pain experienced through the natural processes of competition and adaptation.

Wes: Really? You're going to express concern for how our readers might evaluate my faith because of my curiosity about Buddhism, and then you're going to throw evolution on the table?

Milton: Ha! You know what I mean. People may disagree with the details of evolution, but there's no question that life forms advance based on suffering. Without pain, life just muddles along.

Wes: You're making a good point. But what I find even more remarkable, regardless of the metaphor, is that the Randalls of the world make their ways toward peace without having to adopt this or that theological metaphor. Should it be a bit disturbing to those of us with advanced degrees that Randall is moving to that place without going on any long meditation retreats, attending courses on mystical spiritual formation, or seeking the guidance of a spiritual director?

Milton: You're suggesting that God may not need our brilliance in order to keep the redemptive plan on course?

Wes: It's a rather troubling thought, isn't it?

> *Interested readers can continue the dialogue with us on our Wordpress blog:* **jobinthewhirlwind.com**

About the Authors

Milton Horne is professor of religion at William Jewell College, Liberty, Missouri, where he has taught in the religion department since 1986.

Wes Eades is a pastoral counselor and marital therapist in private practice, living in Waco, Texas while Skyping with a few clients from places far away.

Made in the USA
San Bernardino, CA
11 October 2014